EMPATH

SEEING THE WORLD DIFFERENTLY

Subtitle: Discover the Secrets To Becoming An Empowered Empath Through Self-Healing and Emotional Regulation

MARLEY HENDRIX

Table of Contents

PART I

Chapter 1: The Empath

Imagine standing next to somebody on the street. You don't know them, nor have you have any type of communication with them. However, you can sense that this person is not doing well. They are sad and hurting on the inside. You don't understand why they have these feelings, but you know that they do because you can feel them within yourself too. This may sound like a far-fetched reality, but it's not. This is something that occurs when an individual is an empath.

Empathy means that you have the ability to sense and feel what someone is going through fully. This goes a step further than what we have already described in the first three chapters. While a highly sensitive person can understand and even relate to the emotions around them, an empath actually has the ability to feel those emotions within themselves. For example, if someone near an empath is sad and depressed, the empath will feel it inside of them as if they are standing in that person's shoes.

Dr. Judy Orloff, who is a professor of psychiatry at UCLA and a pioneer in the field of empathy, suggests that while highly sensitive people still have a barrier towards the stimulation in the environment, an empath has no filter, so absorbs everything around them like a sponge in a bowl of water. This makes it very hard for empaths to protect themselves and their emotions. They are also very sensitive sounds, strong personalities, and busy environments. They basically feel everything to a very high degree, and one of the reasons they become overwhelmed is because they cannot decipher or separate the emotions from their own. This means that as the emotions are coming in, like sadness, happiness, or anger, they have a hard time telling if they are feeling that way, or someone close to them is.

How To Tell If You're An Empath

There are many unique traits that empaths possess. The following are some of these qualities. If these sound familiar to you, then you may be an empath too.

- They are world-class nurturers and naturally giving. If you want someone by your side through thick and thin, then an empath is your person to go to.
- They are highly attuned to the environment around them, to the point that they feel everything down to their core. They might as well be standing inside of a person's body because they are feeling their emotions so closely.
- They are uncomfortable in large crowds because they are being inundated with all of the thoughts and feelings surrounding them, which can become very overwhelming and very exhausting.
- As a result of being uncomfortable in large crowds, empaths are often introverts. They usually prefer one-on-one interactions, rather than being in groups settings of any sort.
- Since it is draining for them to be around so many people, empaths need their alone time to help them recharge.

- They love nature as it nourishes and restores them. An empath would rather walk on a nice hiking trail than a city block.

- They have very finely tuned senses, so they are very sensitive to smells, noise, and excessive talking. If you touch an empath, don't be surprised if they jump a little bit.

- Since empaths can deeply feel the pain in others, they try very hard to relieve that pain for them, even if it's at their own expense.

The last person an empath thinks about is themselves. This is unfortunate because they are the ones who usually need the most care. While empaths have very appealing personalities on the surface, they often go through a lot of suffering because of the innate qualities they possess. The focus of this chapter will be the negative factors that come from having empathic traits.

Problems That Empaths Deal With

With all of the attributes that empaths have, they are bound to run into problems when dealing with the real world. While many people can separate themselves from others, it is nearly impossible for an empath to do the same. They are constantly sucked into the trials and tribulations of society, and as a result, are constantly dealing with significant emotional issues.

Empaths are often misunderstood. People who are not in their position cannot fathom what is going on in their minds. However, an empath is burdened with so many things that it becomes hard for their mind to cope with everything. If you know an empath or are one yourself, then you know exactly what I am talking about. The following are some of the challenges that these individuals have to deal with.

Their Feelings Can Be Flipped Easily

Imagine having the best day of your life. You are happy, energetic, and don't have a care in the world. You are on top of everything, and it seems that nothing can bring you down. Well, that is until something does. Of course, anyone of our moods can change quickly when something happens directly to us. This is not impossible. For an empath, though, nothing needs to happen to them directly. Once they are in the presence of someone who is emotionally distraught, their joyous mood can switch to a depressing mood instantly. Empaths are constantly shifting between various emotions due to the strong sensitivity they have with the environment. This puts them on a constant emotional rollercoaster. If they are in a group, the emotional fluctuations are even greater. From moment to moment, an empath will never know what his mood will be.

Emotional Fatigue Is Real

Dealing with our own emotions can be exhausting. Now, imagine adding several other people's emotions and having them be all over the spectrum. This can create heavy emotional fatigue.

Compassion Becomes A Burden

Empaths are often ridiculed for caring too much about other people. The truth is, it is hard for them to be any other way. They cannot turn off the compassion meter, which can become a burden after a while. Since an empath can feel suffering more than anyone else around them, it is difficult to not feel responsible for remedying it.

People Not Understanding Their Needs

Empaths are very likable, so people enjoy being around them. Many of them get invited out a lot. However, empaths need their alone time once in a while to recharge, but most people do not understand that. They believe they are just flaking on them, so they push them, even more, to go out. Unfortunately, most empaths will give in because they do not want to upset their friends.

Needing Time To Process Transitions

Empaths will have a hard time jumping from a high-stimulus to a low-stimulus environment. If they go from a crowded event to a small event, they will feel hollow for a while, trying to process the change. On the other hand, going into a suddenly crowded environment will overwhelm them.

It Can Be hard To Enjoy Yourself

Since you are always inundated with other people's feelings, it can be hard to enjoy yourself. You feel bad about feeling good, essentially, because you know that other people are suffering.

Get Taken Advantage Of

Because empaths care so much about other people, they often get taken advantage of. Certain types of people love to pounce on empaths because they know they can get away with a lot. We will talk more about these people later on.

Saying "No" Is Difficult

Empaths often feel guilty for saying "no," even though they need to say it more than anyone else. You are always willing to sacrifice your time and well-being for others until you hit a wall.

The struggles that empaths deal with are real. Unfortunately, their most unique qualities that are beneficial to other people have the most negative impact on them. Empaths must learn to use their characteristics in a way that helps others but does not overwhelm them. Otherwise, they will always live a life of suffrage.

What Creates An Empath

There is a wide range of reasons why a person becomes an empath. Some people are born with this mindset, while others develop it over time. This is the whole nature vs. nurture argument. Dr. Judy Orloff has described four different factors that contribute to empathy and becoming an empath.

- Some infants come out of the womb and are more sensitive to certain stimuli. For example, they cry more often and are extra sensitive to things like sound. Basically, people are born with different temperaments, which suggests that being an empath is a birthright to a degree.

- It is possible that there is a genetic component to being an empath. Many parents who are empaths often give birth to kids who are empaths too. However, this is not always the case, which means our genes are not the sole cause and may not have any connection in some cases.

- Children who are neglected or abused as a child often have their defenses torn down. They have experienced what it's like to be around a lack of sensitivity. In turn, they become extra sensitive as adults.

- Overly supportive parents can also create extra sensitive children. Children who take in many empath traits from their parents will carry them into adulthood.

Many researchers have found a significant amount of scientific backing related to being an empath. There is a specialized group of cells in our brains that are responsible for compassion. They enable everyone to mirror the emotions of the people close to them. These are known as mirror neurons, and they are thought to be hyper-responsive in empaths.

Empaths are also thought to have a stronger emotional contagion. This is a phenomenon where people can pick up on the emotions around them and then start feeling the same way. This can be seen in a room full of infants when one of them begins crying, and it sets off a cascade among the other babies too. Eventually, the whole room of infants is crying.

Finally, empaths are shown to have a higher sensitivity to dopamine, which is a neurotransmitter associated with the pleasure response. Dopamine is generally released when stimulated in some way. When an individual experiences a joyous moment, dopamine is released, which makes them even happier. Due to the higher sensitivity, empaths need less dopamine to increase their mood. This may explain why empaths are content being alone. They do not need a lot of external stimulation to feel good.

In summary, if you are an empath, then it is not something you can avoid. You are essentially stuck being an empath for the rest of your life. As you will see later on, this is not a bad thing. It is imperative, though, to manage the negative aspects of this quality, Which we will also get into more in the next couple of chapters.

Empaths And Toxic Relationships

While most people like empaths, the relationships they are in are not usually reciprocal. Meaning the compassion, kindness, and love that empaths give are not returned to them in the same manner. Of course, an empath would not expect these emotions to be displayed, but it's imperative to point out the lopsided relationships that many of them are involved in.

While many people take advantage of an empaths generosity, certain personality types take it to the extreme. These are the worst individuals for an empath to be around. They are collectively known as energy vampires and come in various forms. If you are an empath, you must recognize these energy suckers do that you can avoid them completely.

Energy vampires are the opposite of empaths. They lack any type of empathy, compassion, or emotional maturity, and do their best to take what they can from people. It is usually not through force, but with various manipulation tactics. Empaths, who are always willing to give, are the perfect victim for them. The following are different types of energy vampires that must be avoided.

The Victim

These vampires are always the martyr. They believe the world is out to get them and take no responsibility for their lives. They continually blame, manipulate, or blackmail to get what they want. The victim vampires feel unworthy in their lives, so they will work to garner sympathy by making you feel guilty.

The Narcissist

The Narcissist has no ability to show empathy and has no genuine interest in other people. They always expect to be put first, no matter the circumstances. They have giant egos that need to be fed, and they will always make sure not to go hungry. Narcissist vampires are dangerous because they will be very likable and charming at first to gain your trust, but then stab you in the back when it benefits them.

The Dominator

The dominator will make themselves feel superior through intimidation, whether physical or emotional. They are often loudmouths with rigid beliefs about how the world should be. Therefore, many of their viewpoints are archaic and can be seen as racist, sexist, or homophobic.

The Judgmental One

Judgmental vampire suffers from low self-worth. As a result, they project these feelings onto other people through shame and ridicule. Basically, they make themselves feel better by making you feel small.

The Innocent One

Unlike the other vampires, the innocent types are usually not malicious. They genuinely need help in their lives and are just looking for a hand. Their intent is not to harm anyone; they are just not emotionally strong enough to help themselves. That being said, you will still drain yourself if you are their constant rock to lean on. The key is to help but also to encourage self-sufficiency.

Unfortunately, many energy vampires are those who are closest to us, like family and lifelong friends. This makes it even easier to fall into their traps and get out energy sucked out by them. This makes it more imperative to be on high alert for their manipulative tactics.

The objective of this chapter was to paint a picture of what an empath is. Hopefully, you can visualize one in your mind. If you are an empath too, then you probably recognize many of the characteristics described here. Also, you have probably experienced the same setbacks. The remaining chapters in this book will focus on the positive aspects of being an empath and how you, as an empath, can share your gifts with the world, while also protecting yourself from harm.

Chapter 2: The Empath Blessing

In the previous chapter, I described in detail what an empath is and what challenges exist from being one. I admit that I probably did not paint the most appealing picture, but my goal was to make you aware of the specific empath traits so that you can recognize them within yourself and others. Once you do, then you can work on improving yourself by overcoming the obstacles that are in the way of your success.

The truth is, being an empath is a blessing because you bring so much value to the world. Some have described their abilities as paranormal, or as having a superpower. People rely on you because of the gifts you possess to be able to help them. The focus of this chapter will be to illustrate the positive impact that an empath can bring to those around them, in every facet of their lives. If you fall into this camp, just know that you are a very good addition to anyone's life.

Empaths As Leaders

Because of the unique personality traits an empath has, they are actually great leaders. They have a strong capability to create positive change within an organization. This is considering they don't allow themselves to be manipulated. The following are some of the top reasons that empaths can become successful leaders in any environment.

- They want to improve the world. Empaths are contributors, rather than takers, and want to improve human relationships by offering tremendous support.

- Empaths burden themselves with other people's issues, which may not be great in the long run, but can get a lot accomplished in real-time. Bearing this extra burden will often push empaths towards their goals.

- They have good relationship skills and can communicate better with those around them because of their deep understanding of the world.

- Their followers do not see them as intimidating, which means they are more willing to work with them.

- Empaths have a deep love for humanity, in general, so they do not discriminate against anybody.

- They look towards the future, not in the sense of making profits, but finding solutions that plague so many people.

- Even the most closed off and difficult people to work with will engage with an empath because they will provide a comfortable atmosphere to do so.

- They do not let success get to their heads, and they will not try to steal all the credit.

While empaths are not known for having strong personalities, they have endearing qualities that make them very likable and trustworthy. People are drawn to empaths, and this allows them to create successful teams with many different types of people. If empaths held more leadership roles, whether, in politics or business, the world might be a friendlier place.

Why Empaths Are Great Friends

Just like highly sensitive people, empaths have appealing personalities that make them great friends. As an empath yourself, just know that anyone is lucky to have you in their lives. Why do empaths make great friends? I will explain why.

Empaths Will Know When You're Not Well

Empaths will know stuff about you without you having to tell them. This is not in a creepy or intrusive way. They simply have the skills to pick up on various clues that you are unknowingly putting out. These abilities go beyond being intuitive and actually border on the paranormal. It is as if they can read your mind. As a result, an empath will know when you are upset, ill, tired, or going through any other negative emotion. There is no hiding your feelings when you are with an empath. Because they recognize the pain you are going through; they will have the compassion and understanding to help you get through it. If you have a problem, you can always count on your empath friend.

They Know The Right Things To Say

Because empaths are so good at picking up on the emotions of others, you rarely have to explain to them what you are going through. The chances are, they already know. This will save you a lot of pain and frustration, trying to explain what is wrong. Of course, if you want to explain it, an empath will listen with open ears.

When we are feeling negative, for whatever reason, it can be hard to get the point across to people because they are not going through our experiences. They are not living in our bodies. An empath will be by your side and will not ask unusual questions or completely miss the point about what you're saying. Finally, they will understand when to push forward with an issue and when to back off. In most cases, an empath will know what to say and the right time to say it.

They Can Protect You From Other People

There is something ironic to discuss here. Since empaths have such high compassion and kindness inside of them, they are willing to help almost anybody. On the other hand, an empath can help protect you from other toxic people. Because of their ability to understand people quickly, they can determine if a person is genuine or might have some ulterior motives. Therefore, if an empath has some unpleasant vibes about someone, it is in your best interest to listen.

Some people suggest not to be around anyone that an empath does not approve of. I will not go that far. However, never dismiss the feelings of an empath and always keep them in the back of your mind. Even if an individual seems perfect in every way, there might be some red flags you miss that an empath will recognize immediately. They will know if someone is dishonest and what their true intentions are. On that note, do not try to be dishonest with an empath because they will pick up on it quickly.

They Are Fun To Be Around

Being friends with an empath is an exciting experience because they are free spirits. They tend not to live in the norm and are always up for an adventure. If you're looking for a travel buddy, consider an empath because they are up for almost anything. You will have a blast. A word of caution: You may have to share your empath friend with other people because their personalities are attractive, even to strangers.

They Are Great Listeners

When you are speaking with an empath, you can be sure they are listening. They are not just listening so they can respond, but because they genuinely want to hear what you are saying. They will also help you come up with the best solutions since they understand you so well. However, if you are just talking to vent and are not looking for someone to solve your problems, an empath will understand that too and just listen without interrupting.

I want you to assess your current situation right now regarding your inner circle. Who are the types of people that you enjoy hanging out with the most? I want you to be completely honest with yourself. What personality traits do they carry? Do some of your best friends behave as empaths, at least partially? The chances are, those whom you genuinely enjoy being around possessed many of the innate attributes that are associated with empaths.

Seek out empath relationships, and you will not be disappointed. If you are an empath, then share your gifts with the world. Just make sure to keep yourself safe. I will discuss how to do this more in the next chapter.

The Empath As A Spouse

For the final showcasing of why being an empath is a blessing, I will discuss why empaths make great spouses. If you can find an empath as a partner, then you will be in a luckier place.

They Care About Making You Happy

With empaths, you do not have to worry about selfishness in a relationship. They want a happy life, and they understand that making their spouse happy is part of it. They are more concerned with having a genuine connection with their partners than they are with material possession.

They Make Amazing Parents

If you want children someday, then having an empath as a partner is a blessing because they make amazing parents. An issue that children deal with is that the adults in their lives don't understand them or pay attention to them. They often feel neglected and tossed aside. This will not be the case with an empath. They will be in tune with their children, just as much as they are with anyone else.

They Are Willing To Change For The Better

As a relationship grows, so must the people who are involved. Some individuals are so hardheaded that they are never willing to change. Empaths are so profoundly connected to the world and the people around them that they will recognize their shortcomings and will always be willing to work on them. If there are issues within a relationship, the empath will look inside of themselves and determine where they need to improve.

They Are More Tolerant And Understanding

Empaths understand that people are not perfect. They can also recognize the pain someone is experiencing on the inside. As a result, they are more patient, tolerant, and understanding of people's mistakes and shortcomings.

They Want You To Be Yourself

You do not have to put on a fake persona for an empath. They want you to be yourself. In fact, if you are trying to be fake, they will pick up on it quickly.

The Love Is Passionate

Empaths know how to make you happy. When they do make you happy, they will feel the same way. This will bring them a lot of joy and passion. The happier you are, the happier they will be. So, they will love you with great passion, and make you feel more accepted than anyone else can.

They Are Great At Working Through Disagreements

Since an empath can put themselves in your shoes, it is easier for them to see where you are coming from. They will be able to respond accordingly and work through disagreements more smoothly.

They Hold You Accountable

This may be one of the most important traits of being an empath. Since empaths really understand what you are going through, they will have compassion, but also know that you have the ability to fix it. As a result, they will hold you accountable for improving yourself and getting past whatever is harming you.

As you can see, an empath is a great leader, friend, partner, and pretty much anything else. As long as they are able to harness their power for the well-being of others while keeping themselves safe, they can do a lot of great things in this world. Don't be a stranger to an empath.

Chapter 3: Protecting Yourself

A knight in shining armor has the power to protect those who need him. However, without his armor, he will be harmed easily. The same holds true for an empath. An empath is a true blessing to the world, as we detailed in the previous chapter. However, without properly protecting themselves, an empath is at great risk for many negative consequences. Their mental and physical health, relationships, careers, and even personal safety can be affected, so they must take the proper precautions for their own well-being.

The focus of this final chapter will be about how an empath can protect themselves. I will go over some valuable tips and strategies to keep you safe so that you can continue to bless the world with your gifts. The reality is, once you burn out, you can no longer help others. This means that self-care is not just for you but also for the benefit of other people. The better you are to yourself, the better you can be to other people.

Protect Yourself Against Energy Vampires

While empaths can recognize a negative person because they are aware of people's true motivations, they still fall victim to toxic individuals. Their caring personalities can get the best of them, so they fall prey to people who use them the most. The obvious example here is energy vampires. These are any type of individuals who literally suck out your energy and make you feel drained. I described energy vampires in an earlier chapter, and now I will go over how to protect yourself as an empath from these energy stealers.

Realize They Exist

The first step in solving a problem is recognizing there is one. Energy vampires are a big problem for you if you are an empath. Empaths have a tendency to believe that all people are good and ignore the fact they are in a toxic relationship. Recall some of the characteristics I described for energy vampires and start realizing that bed people who want to take advantage of you do exist.

Keep A Journal Of Your Gut Instincts

Since empaths are highly intuitive, probably more so than anyone else, their gut instincts will tell them a lot about a person. As an empath, you must learn to listen to your gut instincts and never dismiss them, no matter how ridiculous they may seem at first. Also, after spending a lot of time with energy vampires, you can start losing the ability to believe how you feel. One thing these energy stealers are good at is manipulation.

When you are with someone, pay attention to what they are engaging in and write down how they make you feel inside. Pay special attention to how they treat a variety of people they encounter, like waitresses, flight attendants, and cashiers, etc. How an individual treats people who are not considered high on the status bar says a lot about who they are.

Have A Reality-Check Friend

A friend like this is an objective observer who has not been taken in by the energy vampire. They should be trustworthy and be able to their honest opinion about a person when your own judgment might be clouded.

Pat Yourself On The Back

Empaths often due not give themselves the credit they deserve, even though they are responsible for many of the good things around them. Instead, they deflect the credit onto someone else, effectively minimizing their own contributions. I don't want you to get a big head here, but I hope you can pat yourself on the back often recognize what you have accomplished. Write these accomplishments down on a piece of paper daily, so you have something visual to look at.

Put Yourself First

This should be the case no matter who you encounter in your life, but energy vampires are exceptionally good at making empaths feel guilty. They will use every manipulative tactic in existence to make sure they are at the forefront of your mind. They do not care about you unless you are doing something for them. So, make them stop caring. Whenever you feel like your in the presence of an energy vampire, take a step back. Leave the room completely if you have to. From here, remind yourself about your needs and that you deserve to live a joyful life. This will help keep you from falling into the vampire's trap.

Add "No" To Your Vocabulary

I don't care if you have to stand in front of the mirror all day repeating this word, but get as comfortable as you can saying the word "no." It is okay, and even necessary, to use this word once in a while. Empaths have a difficult time saying "no," and their knee-jerk reaction to anything is often "yes" without even considering their own feeling. I don't want you to automatically say "yes" to everything because you will not have the ability to set boundaries. If you have a hard time saying "no," at first, start with a lighter phrase like, let me think about it. Eventually, you can work yourself up as you feel comfortable. The main goal is t not be agreeable all the time.

Prioritize Your Own Quality Time

Set aside sometime every day for your own needs. Even if it is just 20 minutes, this time should be spent focused on your well-being and self-care. Do whatever makes you feel good at this moment, like meditation, reading, taking a bath, or going for a walk. Avoid things that might bring you stress, like social media drama, or watching the news. Stick to your guns about this self-care time, and do not let anyone interrupt it. Visualize all of your negative energy, disappearing into thin air.

Set Boundaries

Learn to set boundaries with people, or they will take up all of your time. As an empath, people will be vying for your attention because they know you will give it to them. You need to put the breaks on this mindset ASAP. I am not saying you can't help people. However, you need to put strict limits on how much time you will spend doing so, because you still need to fit in your self-care. If your friend needs help, set aside time when you can help them, but also place a strict time limit on the encounter. You cannot just be available any time of day for as long as they need it. This may sound insensitive, but it's really not. Your well-being is important too.

One of the ways to ensure you live a happy life as an empath is to keep toxic people away from you as much as they can. Vampires, like the many I have described, can sniff out the blood of an empath and dominate them into submission. If you are not careful, you will be under their control for the rest of your life. There may be times you cannot avoid toxic people; therefore, the techniques above can be used to distance yourself and avoid their tactics as much as you can.

Take regular stock of your friends too. The people in your inner circle should fill you up and make you feel good. If they are not doing that, then it's time to distance yourself or get rid of people completely. An energy vampire can infiltrate themselves into your life unsuspectedly. You must stay on high alert at all times for these individuals.

Harnessing Your Empath Power

Empaths have strengths that cannot be denied. The world needs these blessings now more than ever. This is why it's important to take care of your inner empath. We cannot afford to lose you. Once empaths learn how to harness their superpowers, they can become empath warriors and begin saving the world. Empaths who know how to save their energy are unstoppable because they know themselves well enough to practice self-care and stop absorbing the negative energy around them.

Going back to Dr. Judy Orloff, as an empath herself and someone who has researched the topic endlessly, she has come up with several strategies to harness your empath power and make you a true warrior in this respect. I encourage you to practice these techniques on a regular basis, so they become a habit for you.

- Express gratitude every day for what you have in life. Being grateful allows your mind to stay focused on positive energy by keeping you in the moment, rather than wasting energy worrying about the future.
- Practice different meditation techniques. There are many techniques out there that can help center you and make you in charge of your emotions.

Mediation can take a while to master, but the initial goal is to reach a state of mindfulness

- Practice mindful breathing by focusing on your inhalation and exhalation. Breath in clarity and strength and breath out stress and negativity. Make sure you can feel your breaths down to your diaphragm. Practice these several times a day.

- Strengthen your intuition by learning to listen to it. Notice when your energy levels either increase or decrease when your around somebody. Stick with the people who make your energy levels go up.

- Practice loving yourself every day. Make sure to always engage in positive self-talk. How you speak to yourself plays a big role in your self-worth.

These exercises are simple and can start being used right away. When they become a regular part of your routine, you will be able to share your empath gifts, without being taken advantage of.

Best Careers For An Empath

To give yourself the best chance of winning, it is imperative to set up an environment that benefits you. You will never stop being an empath, and nor should that be your goal. However, it should be your goal to use your strengths in the best way possible. If you are like most people, then you need to work to make a living. It will behoove you to be in a setting that enhances your strengths and minimizes your weaknesses. The following are some of the best career options for empaths.

Nursing

Nursing would be a great career path for a naturally caring and compassionate person, like an empath. They will be using the skills they possess every day, providing the best care for people. Just be mindful that high-stress and fast-paced settings like the emergency room or the ICU can create some complications for the empath's psyche. However, this can be overcome with some practice and experience.

Artistic Careers

These include things like writing, painting, ceramics, or photography. Empaths are known to be creative individuals, so anything in this line of work will be great for them.

Psychologist Or Counselors

People in these careers need to be intuitive, kind, compassionate, and caring. They need to have a deep desire to help people and often have to read between the lines to get the real answers. An empath possesses all of these qualities, so they would excel in this career path.

Veterinarian

Empaths are not just great with people, but also animals. In fact, there is a subset of empaths who can relate to animals on a very deep level, almost as if they can read their thoughts and communicate with them. This is great since animals cannot speak for themselves. An empath who becomes a vet can help heal and comfort sick animals, and also soothe their worried owners.

Musician

Just like with an artist, an empath can let out their emotions and creativity in this line of work. There will also be opportunities to play so many different instruments, as well.

Teacher

There are very few people who need empathy in their lives more than children. Children cannot always express their needs with clarity, so having someone who understands them well is a huge plus. They will gravitate towards an empath because they feel comfortable around them. With proper motivation and support, a teacher could change a student's entire life.

As an empath, if you are looking for a career where you will thrive and none of the above interests you, that's okay. There are plenty of opportunities out there that will require your skillset. While you can succeed anywhere, jobs that require compassion, care, patience, intuitiveness, and kindness, while also being less fast-paced, might be the best pathways to take.

Being Kind To An Empath

I want to end this book by speaking to those on the opposite side. If you have gotten through this book and realized that you are not an empath, that's okay. The chances are that you know an empath, or will meet one at some point. I want to help you understand some important issues about being an empath so that you can bring the best out of them, and they can bring the best out of you. As I mentioned before, an empath will be one of the best people in your life, if you understand how the dynamics of the relationship will work. Here are a few important facts to remember.

- Empaths cannot change who they are. They can work on ways to protect themselves, so they are not used and abused, but they cannot stop being extra kind, compassionate, and caring.
- Empaths cannot be caged and become shut-ins. They have to get out and explore; otherwise, they will lose their zest for life.

- Empaths need time alone, so make sure they get it.

- They see life much differently than others, so give them support.

- They know if you're lying, so always be honest, even if it hurts.

- They love to laugh, so make them laugh often.

- They will be on an emotional rollercoaster, and so will you.

In summary, do not be with an empath if you can't handle life being different every day. If you can, then get ready for the time of your life.

PART II

Chapter 1: Why So Sensitive?

"For a highly sensitive person, a drizzle feels like a monsoon."

-Anonymous

When something out of the ordinary happens, and it is relatively minor, you may become a little surprised, sad, anxious, or happy, depending on what the situation is. Even though the event happened out of nowhere, it elicits a minor emotional response. This will be the case if your emotional reactions are that of a normal individual. However, if you are part of the subset of the population which is highly sensitive, then your response will be anything but minor.

Imagine going completely over the top with your feelings when something out of the ordinary happens in your life. If you go through a distraught situation, you become much more saddened than those around you. If a friend has something good happen to them, you will act more excited than they do. When someone is loud, you feel it to your core. If this sounds like you, then you might be a highly sensitive person.

Individuals who are highly sensitive display stronger reactivity to external and internal stimuli, whether emotional, physical, or social. They are thought to have deeper sensitivities at the central nervous system. It is estimated that about 15-20 percent of the population falls under this umbrella. Highly sensitive persons are believed to be much more disturbed by violence or tension. If they see something bad happen on the news, they will be distraught and might even be bothered by it the whole day. In contrast, someone who is not in their shoes will just think about it for a moment. On the flip side, if you make them happy, they will be exceptionally excited beyond control. It's how they are built.

This may not sound like a big deal to most. You have probably known several people who are overly emotional. However, this goes beyond just crying a little extra during a movie. If you were to go inside the mind of a highly sensitive person, what you are likely to experience would overwhelm you instantly. If you are living with this mindset, then you know exactly what I am talking about.

Despite what people may think, highly sensitive people are not dramatic for no reason. They often cannot help the way they react in certain situations. At least, not without becoming aware of it first. These individuals will often notice things much more acutely than other people do. This relates especially to the feelings of others. While most individuals will simply overlook the pain and suffering of someone else, a highly sensitive person will be more aware of their emotions. They may not know exactly what is wrong, but just that something is okay. They will pick up on the subtleties of body language, facial expressions, and tone of voice.

Even if they don't know an individual, they will be in-tune with the vibes the person puts off. All sensitivity radars will be off the charts.

How To Tell If You're In The Camp

If you have always felt a little different than everybody else around you, then you might be dealing with a highly sensitive personality. Of course, there are many different attributes to consider before knowing for sure. The following are some of the signs of being in this camp. Once you understand whether you're a highly sensitive person or not, then we can proceed forward.

- You are extremely unsettled by cruelty or violence. While most people don't enjoy violence, a highly sensitive person will become extremely disturbed or physically ill by it, even if they don't see it personally.
- You are frequently emotionally exhausted because of how others feel. Essentially, other people and their feelings have a deep impact on you.
- Time crunches make you extremely anxious and overwhelmed. While approaching deadlines can make anyone's hair get raised, it is exponentially greater for a highly sensitive person.
- You enjoy going int solitude at the end of the day to reduce your stimulation levels.
- You are very jumpy and become frightened quickly.

- You are a very deep thinker. You often reflect on your life and experiences to process everything. You will also play events in your head over and over again.

- You seek to find answers to life's questions and wonder why things are the way they are.

- You are startled easily by sudden, loud noises.

- You have reduced pain tolerance.

- You have a rich inner world. You probably grew up with many imaginary friends and might still have them as an adult. You frequently go into a fantasy world.

- You are extremely upset by change, whether positive or negative. It can really throw you off.

- You are very sensitive to the environmental stimuli around you, like the birds chirping, sirens, new smells, or unusual sites. This is because all of your senses are heightened.

- When you're hungry, you become angry too.

- You hate conflict and disagreements. You want people to get along and not fight with each other. You definitely avoid confrontation if you can.

- You are very thin-skinned. You do not take criticism well, whether it is constructive or not.

- You're very conscientious of making mistakes. You're not perfect, but you try extremely hard to be.

- The beauty of your surroundings moves you deeply. Whether it is artwork, a rich scent, or a delicious looking meal, you are enthralled by all of it.
- You will compare yourself to others and often feel inferior as a result.
- You are very perceptive and insightful. You pick up on things that others don't.

If you have been dealing with the issue of being highly sensitive, then you have probably been looked down upon your whole life. People may have told you to toughen up, be less sensitive, or grow a backbone. Don't take any of these statements personally because these individuals did not know better. In fact, you may not have known better and thought there was something wrong with you. Well, as you read further, you will actually begin to understand your unique gifts.

What Makes People Overly Sensitive?

There are many factors to consider when deciding on why you are a highly sensitive person. If having these feelings is an anomaly for you, meaning it's not your normal personality, then it is probably a unique life event that is causing you to behave in this manner. For example, losing a loved one, having poor health, not eating properly, or getting a lack of sleep may contribute to feelings of over sensitivity. However, if you have always been this way, then it goes well-beyond life events. It is ingrained in you to be a highly sensitive person.

Children who were severely criticized, bullied, or went through some type of abuse or trauma can also end up being highly sensitive. Their psyches took a major hit while they were children, so they grew up to be unsure of themselves, which may have contributed to their over-sensitivity, as a result.

Your highly sensitive feelings are likely to have a genetic component to them. So, you might have been born this way as it was passed on through your genes. Also, environmental and social factors may be involved. If your parents, or those you grew up around, were highly sensitive people, then you might have picked up on their personality traits and acquired them as your own. Of course, you can also end up completely opposite from your parents and other influential people, so their attributes may not mean anything in relation to you.

Overall, a highly sensitive person is thought to have a brain that is wired differently, so it has a lower threshold for the environment. So, any type of stimulus will have an exponential effect on them. Many of these characteristics can be seen in babies, as some infants are much more emotional and sensitive to things like sound. This further suggests that people are born highly sensitive, rather than made. In the mid-1990s, husband and wife psychology duo, Arthur and Elaine Aron, coined the term "sensory-processing sensitivity," which is the official scientific phrase used to describe a highly sensitive person. Through their research, the husband and wife duo stated further that the nervous system of someone with sensory-processing sensitivity had variations in their nervous system that was different from others who did not display highly sensitive qualities.

Negative Aspects Of Being A Highly Sensitive Person

Being in the camp of high sensitivity can certainly have their advantages, which we will go over in the next chapter. For now, I will discuss the negative aspects of being a highly sensitive person. This personality trait can impact every area of your life, and if you are not careful, it can create a lot of pain and suffering in the long run. Unfortunately, people will take advantage of the kind qualities of a sensitive individual, and the results are not always pleasant.

In The Workplace

If you are like the majority of people in the world, then you probably spend much of your time in the workplace. Here, you will have regular interactions with your coworkers and those in upper management. While certain things in the workplace may be a slight struggle or annoyance for most individuals, a highly sensitive person may have their whole workflow and mood affected in a significant way. The following are certain obstacles that only a highly sensitive person would understand and contend within the workplace.

- A strong aroma in the office can completely throw off a highly sensitive person. These can be smells that come from different foods or from someone wearing a lot of perfume.

- Other sensory issues like bright colors or loud sounds in the workspace, can severely affect their focus and ability to do their job.

- Trying to complete last-minute deadlines without proper planning can cause a highly sensitive person to become overwhelmed quickly. This is definitely not when they do their best work.

- Criticism from a boss or employee can truly mess with a highly sensitive person's head. They may even react in an unorthodox fashion, like having a mental breakdown, crying excessively, or running out of the office. They often cannot help it as it is an instantaneous reaction.

- Highly sensitive people will have a hard time speaking up and asking for what they want or need. They hate rocking the boat and definitely don't want to upset anyone else. As a result, they are often overlooked for many opportunities.

- These individuals are often seen as weak and ineffectual, so people will walk all over them. The highly sensitive person will usually let them.

- They are usually overstressed, even if it's a normal workday with nothing unusual going on. Anything in their environment can make them feel this way. Remember that highly sensitive people are more prone to be affected by environmental stimuli.

- There will be constant comparison with coworkers, and the highly sensitive person will always feel like they come up short.
- Wearing professional clothes, like ties, high-heels, or various other things that are uncomfortable, are highly bothersome to you.

As a highly sensitive person, you must be aware of these unique traits and how they will make you react. Otherwise, your experience at work will become constant suffrage.

In Their Personal Lives

Highly sensitive people will also deal with others in their personal lives, both at home and in various relationships. Their personality traits will often not do them any favors in this aspect of their lives, either. As a highly sensitive person, you will have extremely emotional and sometimes hostile relationships with those close to you. The following are some issues you may run into.

- Highly sensitive people will sense when their friends and family are going through some issues. They will also allow these emotions to overwhelm them.
- If a highly sensitive person gets asked to do something, in most cases, they will say yes, no matter how busy their schedule is or what they have planned. Saying no is a true challenge.
- These individuals are their own worst critic and will be excessively hard on themselves for something, while easily forgiving someone else for the same issues.
- They are often poor with self-care because they are too busy worrying about others.

- They are more sensitive to trouble and conflict within a relationship. They will become stressed easily during a conflict.
- They will have a lot of self-doubt about their abilities, which will show in their personal relationships. They will usually be the ones to submit and compromise full.
- They will have a hard time asking their friends for anything.
- It will be very easy to hurt a highly sensitive person's feelings. Plus, they can be manipulated easily.

As you can see, a highly sensitive person will not have an easy time with their personal relationships. They will usually be the givers and never the takers. These qualities can wear down on them and create much emotional and psychological harm if not dealt with accordingly.

Now that we have a picture of what a highly sensitive person is, you probably have a pretty good idea if you are one or not. We will get into more detail about the positive qualities of this personality trait.

Chapter 2: Embrace Your Sensitivities

I know I was pretty hard on highly sensitive people in chapter one and did not paint them in the most positive light. It is hard to imagine that these individuals actually have positive qualities. However, just because a highly sensitive person has flaws and weaknesses does not mean they don't have significant strengths too. In this section, I will go over the reasons why being a highly sensitive person is a good thing and how people can start embracing this aspect of themselves.

Benefits Of Being a Highly Sensitive Person

There are actually many great qualities to being a highly sensitive person, and the world is lucky to have individuals like this. Sensitivity is falsely depicted as being undesirable, which you have probably noticed in your own life. I am here to tell you that it is not a negative trait to have. With all of the controversy surrounding it, the benefits are often overlooked. But, they cannot be ignored any longer.

Having A Depth Of Experience And Feelings

Experiencing the world with heightened emotions gives you a deeper meaning in everything around you. You learn to find joy in the smallest things, which means you have the ability to find good in every area of life. You learn to experience life in a totally different way as a highly sensitive person and notice beauty in the subtleties of life.

Self-Awareness

Self-awareness means having a strong sense of who you are and where you belong in the world. A highly sensitive person has a keen self-awareness. They are hyper tuned in to their emotions, and the reactions that follow them. While a highly sensitive person understands their high levels of emotional volatility, they eventually realize that other people do not process feelings in the same manner that they do. What throws their minds for a loop, will barely be a blip on the radar for someone else.

Intuitive Nurturing Skills

The highly sensitive person is naturally good at nurturing others. Because of their ability to feel deeply, they have a strong desire to bring happiness to other people. They have the instinct to care for others and will support them, so they feel loved and appreciated.

A Knack For Forming Close relationships

Highly sensitive people may take a while to open up to somebody, but once they do, they form strong bonds in the process. They will become the best companions a person can have. The reason highly sensitive people are choosy with making friends is because they can feel the energy of others around them. If the energies don't mesh, they know the relationships won't be a good fit.

Highly sensitive people are not interested in casual acquaintances, but in developing meaningful relationships. They want to be around individuals who make them feel comfortable.

Highly sensitive people are also highly sensitive to things that bring them joy. This means they can find joy in even the smallest things in life. If they are having a bad day, hearing a good song on the radio can completely change their mood.

Why Highly Sensitive People Make Great Friends

As we move through life, we meet and develop relationships with many different people. While we get along and also get to know these individuals well, how many of them truly become great friends? It is rare to find friends who understand us for who we are, leave us feeling warm and make us believe that we are important. A highly sensitive person is a friend who has all of these abilities. These individuals become the best kinds of friends because of the attributes they possess. The following are a few reasons why a highly sensitive person should be a sought-after relationship in your life.

- They are able to manage conflicts well because they have the ability to observe and quickly diffuse a situation. Plus, they have a keen eye for details and can often sense a conflict erupting before it starts.
- They highly understand the needs of others and will work hard to keep their friends happy, including you.

- They like to involve others and help them grow. Even when you make a mistake, they will help you learn from it and maintain your confidence.
- They are not stuck in their own worlds.
- They have a sense of purpose and want to make a difference in people's lives.

If you are a highly sensitive person, know that you can be a great and valuable friend to many people out there.

Why Highly Sensitive People Make Great Employees

While highly sensitive people can struggle in major ways in many work environments, they actually make great employees. The attributes they have make them reliable, hardworking, intuitive, and great team players. Rarely will they cause drama. In fact, they will do their best to avoid it.

Highly sensitive people are often undervalued in the workplace. They are not the most charismatic or outspoken people in the office. In fact, they are probably the ones you will hear from the least. Unfortunately, the soft skills they bring to the table do not get the same recognition as the stronger skills. This does not mean they are less valuable as employees, though. The following are some of the reasons highly sensitive people are a great addition to any company.

- They are the ones you can count on. They have the right attitude, will always show up, and will put in the effort needed to get the job done.

- They are careful decision-makers and will rarely take action hastily. As a result, the decisions they make are often the best possible under the circumstances at the moment.

- If they are in a positive environment, they will thrive beyond your imagination.

- They can be creative and, therefore, find the right solutions to problems.

- People often think that leaders have to be loud and brash. Actually, this is the opposite of what a leader should be. True leaders are intuitive, listen well, and inspire others. This is why a highly sensitive person actually makes a great leader.

- Highly sensitive people will focus on what benefits the team, rather than what benefits themselves.

If you are a highly sensitive person, know that your attributes are truly desired in the workplace, even if it doesn't seem that way.

Guess what? As a highly sensitive person, you are special and bring a unique gift to this world. Too many people are stuck in their own heads and have no concept or understanding of the world around them. You, on the other hand, can acknowledge the thoughts and feelings of other people. Because of your great attributes, you must stop believing that you are undesirable or weak. You are actually the strong one. The next chapter will discuss how you can start believing in yourself and the value that you bring to the world. You will become a better person overall.

Chapter 3: Living As A Highly Sensitive Person

The key to living a happy life as a highly sensitive person is to embrace the good qualities that you possess and showcase them to the world, while not allowing your flaws to control you. The bad part about highly sensitive people is that their oversensitivity gets the best of them, and often at the most inopportune times. The goal of this chapter will be to focus on controlling your emotions and allowing your unique gifts to shine through by using specific action steps to rewire your brain and way of thinking. Mindset shifts will be a major factor in managing your habits and sensitivities. Once you go through the practices and action steps I discuss here; you will truly be able to live your best life as a highly sensitive person.

The first step in the process is realizing who you are. In the previous two chapters, I detailed the positive and negative attributes of a highly sensitive person. In the end, while having this trait has extreme downsides, the positives outweigh the negatives. If you have come to realize that you are a highly sensitive person, then it's time to move on to the strategies and actions steps to manage your emotions.

How To Overcome Your Sensitivities

Just to be clear, you will never get rid of your sensitivities. They have always been a part of who and always will be. The objective is to manage these sensitivities, so you can overcome them. If they control you, they can become a major obstacle. The key is to use them to your advantage by controlling them. The following are some survival tips for highly sensitive people so that they don't become overwhelmed.

- Get plenty of sleep. Usually, 7-8 hours is recommended, but whatever it takes t make you feel well-rested. A lack of sleep will make you irritable, moody, less productive, and decrease your concentration. Proper sleep will help soothe your senses.

- Eat healthy food throughout the day. People dismiss how much of an effect diet has on your mood. But, if you eat foods high in cholesterol, saturated fats, and sugars, you will become tired, irritable, and overly sensitive to stimuli.

- A good pair of headphones can keep you from getting triggered with loud noises. You cannot control the noise, but you can manage how much it affects you.

- Plan time to decompress. Being on the go all the time will always keep you on heightened alert. This means you will continuously be in a frazzled state of mind. Taking time to decompress, preferably at night, can allow your nerves to calm down and no longer be affected by external stimuli. Whatever you can do to isolate yourself from the craziness of the world, do it.

- Give yourself the time and space to get things done. Highly sensitive people do not do well with a packed schedule, so avoid getting yourself in this position if you can help it.

- Limit your caffeine intake. Caffeine is a natural stimulant that will make you feel jittery if taken in excess. Highly sensitive people might be even more sensitive to caffeine. If you drink two cups of coffee a day, cut it down to one.

- Try to avoid excessively lighted areas if you can. In your home, keep your lights dim, as well.

- Get your errands done during the off-hours. This means going out opposite the average person's regular schedule. Get your shopping done during the week, go out with friends on weeknights, and go to the gym early in the morning. The goal here is to avoid huge crowds that can stir up your emotions.

- Get out in nature as much as possible and get away from the hustle-and-bustle of the city.

Even though you are born being highly sensitive, there are still many environmental factors that can trigger you to become more over the top. The survival tips above are meant to prevent overloading your hypersensitive senses. Many psychologists and research scientists have stated that a proper lifestyle may not change our genetics, but it can keep it from making our issues worse.

Having Self-Esteem As A Highly Sensitive Person

Te thing that highly sensitive people struggle with the most is their self-esteem, which is the value and worth they place on themselves. This is because they allow their environment, including the people, around them, to dictate their emotions. It is difficult for these individuals to break away from the feeling other people are having. As a highly sensitive person yourself, it's time for you to start realizing the importance of self-esteem and begin to recognize ways you can improve your own. It is time to stop thinking you are not good enough. The following strategies will take a lot of practice, but once you start implementing them, you will notice major changes in your mindset.

Accept Thoughts, Emotions, And Sensations As They Are

All of these aspects are a part of you but do not define you. They are fleeting in nature and are changing from moment to moment. If you are feeling pain, whether emotional or physical, for a definitive moment, that does not mean you are weak. It is a sensation you are going through that will eventually pass. Instead of letting your thoughts and feeling control you, work on observing them objectively and then letting them go. Do not allow them to become attached to you.

Eliminate The Word "Should" From Your Vocabulary

When you use the word "should," it will elicit a sense of guilt inside of you. If you change it to "could," then you subconsciously open up your mind about what you could be doing and uses less judgment. Using the word "could" also showcases that there are many different options for us, and we are not required to stay on one path. Try it out:

"I should be going to the gym." Change it to, "I could be going to the gym." See the difference?

Do Not Rely On Other People For Self-Esteem

Unfortunately, as highly sensitive people, most of our self-worth is dependent on what other people think of us. You will never place true value on yourself if this is the mindset you will carry. The major problem is that when our outside source for self-esteem vanishes, then the opinion we have of ourselves plummets. We have to internalize our power to create our value and become the sole person who is in charge of it.

Forgive

We all have something in our past that we are not proud of. We must learn to forgive ourselves for the mistakes we made so we can move on. We need to apply the same compassion for ourselves that we tend to show other people. The next time you are hard on yourself, imagine one of your best friends standing in your position. Now, picture what you would tell this person if they made the same mistakes you did. If it's something favorable, then tell yourself the same thing. Stop being your worst critic.

Take Stock Of Your Talents

We tend to focus on our faults, and this severely lowers our self-esteem. We do not give ourselves enough credit by doing this. It is time to take stock of your talents and remember the gifts that you bring to the world. Identify what you are good at. If you are having a tough time coming up with something, then start small. Perhaps you are good at putting things away. This is a good start. As you come up with things, write them down and keep them to look at constantly. Another exercise you can do is write down what you think you're not good at and then crumble up that piece of paper and throw it away. Focus on your positive attributes.

Remember that these exercises will take a lot of consistency. Do not just quit after one day. When you begin incorporating these strategies into your daily life, you will see vast improvements with your mindset.

Focusing On Jobs, You Are Good At

I discussed in the previous chapter about highly sensitive people being model employees. This is still true. However, the goal is to make yourself as happy as possible, and this means avoiding things that will trigger your sensitivities. That being said, there are certain environments and job types where a highly sensitive person will fit in better and even thrive. If you can avoid the stress altogether, then why not do so? The following are the best career options for you if you are a highly sensitive person.

Caring Professions

Careers that require a lot of caring and compassion will be right up a highly sensitive person's alley. These jobs include things like nursing, medicine, counseling, therapy, and coaching. These fields will target a highly sensitive person's strength. Bear in mind that certain areas, like the emergency department or the ICU, may be challenging areas for you. Also, any busy environment will have a lot of different emotions that you will have to contend with. Good options in these fields may be things like home health nursing or individual counseling.

Creative Endeavors

Highly sensitive people are often very creative, so they will thrive in professions where they can show off their creativity. Some of these roles include graphic designer, writer, photographer, artist, or architect. Many creative jobs can be done on a freelance basis, which allows you to create your own schedule. This will be a major benefit to you as a highly sensitive person.

Clergy

If you have a spiritual side to you, then working as a clergy person may be right for you. Bear in mind, that depending on the denomination, you may have to follow strict rules. This may cause difficulty if you are a highly open-minded person. Of course, if you can get over the structure, then your intuition and sensitivity will be valued and accepted.

Academia

With academia, you get to spend a significant amount of time doing thoughtful and intensive research on a subject you have an interest in. In addition, you get to teach your extensive knowledge to students; as a highly sensitive person, you will thrive in your areas. In the end, you are doing meaningful work throughout your profession.

IT Professional

Coding is a major portion of IT and requires a lot of creativity to be successful. You will also need strong intuition and an eye for detail. These are all qualities that are possessed by highly sensitive people. As one of these individuals, software engineering or website development might be the perfect career paths for you.

When choosing a career to go into, you should focus on your strengths and what areas you will be compatible with. Consider your strengths as a highly sensitive person and determine what line of work fits you best.

Dealing With Hyperarousal

There will be times when you are in a state of hyperarousal, where you will be wired up and out of control, physically and mentally. In some cases, hyperarousal can be a defense mechanism, like with the fight-or-flight response. In these moments, being on high alert is a necessity. However, when the hyperarousal goes beyond defined moments, you will be dealing with many problems, including stress, anxiety, and overall diminished emotional and physical health. Yes, being in a state of constant arousal is detrimental to your physical health. Prolonged stress has led to many chronic illnesses, like heart disease, stroke, diabetes, and even some cancers. In addition, mental health disorders like depression are also a possibility.

When you are in the hyperarousal state, you will have an increased heart rate, faster breathing, quicker reflexes, perspiration, and heightened sensitivity to stimuli. So, when you hear a loud noise, you will immediately jump into action, or at least be ready to. Once again, short-term physiological responses like these are not dangerous. If you are consistently in this state, then we have a problem that must be addressed.

Hyperarousal needs to be dealt with quickly; otherwise, it will take over your life. This response is a symptom of another problem, so if you can figure out that problem is, then you can address it directly. The following are some action steps that will have a favorable response to being wired.

Practice Mindfulness

The purpose of this technique is to sit peacefully and consciously observe the chaos and frantic thoughts going on inside your mind without trying to change them, escape from them, or fight them off. Many therapists use this technique with their clients because it is effective in getting over feelings of panic. It also helps to reduce your hyperarousal symptoms.

Perform this technique for about 1-5 minutes at a time. Just sit quietly and focus on your feelings of discomfort, agitation, and anxiety. Concentrate very hard in this area. See if you can visualize these negative feelings and imagine holding them in your arms. A common practice that therapists have their clients do is picture the problems they are holding as being much bigger and worse. It may sound confusing, but it works well for their clients. It is likely because once they've imagined the issue being worse, the thing does not seem as major.

Make Small Achievable Goals Towards Relaxation And Calmness

I do mean to make these goals achievable by keeping them small. When you first start out, shoot for 30 seconds of pure relaxations. Once you achieve this milestone, then try for one minute, then two minutes, and so on. Eventually, you will be able to be in this state for several minutes with no problems. Just work your way up.

It does not matter what relaxation techniques you use, as long as you are in a state of physical relaxation and calmness. This can mean lying down in bed, sitting in a comfortable chair, or meditating. The choice is yours. From here, remain quiet and focus on a body part that feels tense. Now, take one breath in slowly over a few seconds, then hold it for a few seconds before letting it out slowly. As you release the breath, imagine the tension leaving that part of the body you focused on earlier. Truly visualize the tension dissipating like a cloud of smoke.

Evaluate yourself after this. Did your breathing and pulse rate decrease? Do you feel less tense and anxious? If so, then the practice was a success. Keep working on this step to make yourself better.

Positive Self-Talk

In the middle of frantic self-talk that is negative, interrupt yourself and begin saying some encouraging phrases. These include statements like, "You will get through this," or "You are strong and will overcome." This technique will trick your mind and shift it from positive to negative. As a result, you will slow down your pace. Once you do this often, it will become a habit.

Investigate The Root Cause

The above exercises are beneficial; however, you should also determine what the root cause of your hyperarousal is. If you can figure this out, then the risk of flareups in the future will go down. Some of the causes include anxiety, PTSD, excess caffeine, and drug or alcohol use. Once you've narrowed it down, then you can focus on more specific techniques to eliminate the root cause.

For example, Cognitive Behavioral Therapy, or CBT, can be an effective strategy from anxiety. The goal of CBT is to challenge your current thought patterns through talk therapy. The following are a few key steps to make CBT work for you.

- Identify what you are thinking by actually writing them down on something. This way, you can visualize them.
- Assess your thoughts and realize that they may not be true or accurate. We often think negative thoughts for so long that we automatically assume they identify us, and we never challenge them.
- Replace these harmful thoughts with more positive and encouraging ones. Write down all of these new thoughts, as well.
- Now, read these new thoughts to yourself over and over again. Do this until it becomes a habit for you to think of these thoughts, which could take days or weeks.

CBT is a strategy that works for many different disorders, and therapists use it often.

The bottom line to all of this is that you will always be a highly sensitive person. It is not something you can avoid, nor should you try to do so. Despite the challenges that may exist, being a highly sensitive person is still a unique gift that you should embrace every day. Learning the techniques to control your thoughts and emotions, and not allowing your environment to overwhelm, you will ensure that you live a happy and satisfying life. Your sensitivity and intuitiveness are a true gift for many people.

PART III

Chapter 4: Essentials of the Seven Chakras

The seven energy centers of the body, labeled by Eastern spiritual traditions as the "chakras" are located in various places along the spine, ending in the brain. They are strongly tied with emotions, instincts, the experience of consciousness, and the experience of love. Each chakra represents a specific area of the human existence and levels of physical, spiritual, emotional, and psychological balance. In order to apply any of the chakra balancing techniques, it is crucial to understand the concept that human beings are composed of pure energy—the same energy that courses through all other things on earth. Although there are different methods for balancing each chakra individually, there are several commonalities in the process of chakra balancing. When a chakra is considered "out of balance," that means that energy has become trapped somehow, which can cause emotional, psychological, physical, or spiritual blockages that can manifest as a variety of health problems. The level of balance of each chakra is believed to correspond to human actions, feelings, health, and general orientation in the world. In this chapter, we will be breaking down each of the seven chakras and what part they play in the whole of human existence.

Crown Chakra

Color: Auric white or violet

Location: Top of the head

Basic Description: Sometimes called by the Sanskrit name "Sahasrara" or "thousand petals," the crown chakra is known as the chakra, which connects to transcendence, consciousness, and connection with the infinite. The location at the top of the head seems to elongate this chakra to the higher source, and all that lies beyond our daily distractions and ideologies. The Crown chakra works closely with the pituitary and pineal glands, as well as the hypothalamus to regulate the endocrine system. This chakra impacts the brain and nervous system and, therefore, can have very direct impacts on a person's state of mental health.

In Balance: When the Crown chakra is well balanced, people are likely to experience feelings of bliss, unity with all that exists, and transcendence in which all limitations are no more. They will feel fully present and aware of the sacred nature of all of life. They become aware of all that lies beyond the constraints of space and time and draw closer in every moment to pure spiritual ecstasy, divinity, and universal consciousness.

Out of Balance: Imbalances of the Crown chakra can manifest psychologically as schizophrenia and delusion, depression, insomnia, and Alzheimer's. On a physical level, it can cause nerve pain, chronic headaches, and disorders of the thyroid and pineal glands. Emotionally, it can manifest as disconnection from the body, the earth, and the spirit, over obsession with spiritual matters, a cynical attitude, isolating oneself from others, and general close mindedness. It can cause a general inability to set or follow through on goals and produce a feeling of lack of direction in life.

Third Eye Chakra
Color: Indigo

Location: Brows; between the eyes on the forehead

Basic Description: Sometimes called by the Sanskrit "Ajna," meaning "perceiving," this chakra is the center of human intuition, as well as human imagination. This energy center is driven by foresight and openness to life.

In Balance: When the Third Eye chakra is in balance, the rest of the chakras are likely to be well-balanced as well. This is because the Third Eye chakra is seen as a culmination of all other elements in their most pure and balanced form. According to yogic metaphysics, a balanced Third Eye chakra allows for people to transcend the "I" concept and begin to see themselves as deeply connected to the rest of the world, as opposed to separate from it.

Out of Balance: Imbalances in the Third Eye chakra are less likely to manifest psychologically than imbalances of the crown chakra are. However, an imbalanced Third Eye chakra can lead to extreme physical side effects. The relationship to the pituitary gland and general neurological function can lead to decreased metabolism, weakened ability to fight infection, and insomnia. Additionally, a person suffering from an imbalanced Third Eye chakra may experience high blood pressure, seizures, chronic sinusitis, poor vision, migraines, or sciatica. At the most extreme level of imbalance and physical unhealthiness, stroke or blindness can occur. Emotionally, an imbalanced Third Eye chakra may manifest as increased self-doubt and loss of direction in life. People will lose touch with their intuition and, therefore, completely lose sight of their understanding of life and their visions for themselves. They may become paralyzed in moments from the past or terror at what the future may hold.

Throat Chakra
Color: Blue/lavender

Location: Base of the throat

Basic Description: Sometimes called by the Sanskrit name "Vishudda" ("purification"), the throat chakra serves as a passageway between the head and the lower parts of the human body. The primary function of this chakra is self-expression and the art of communication with others. This communication and self-expression generally happen through sound—the vibrations of which can be experienced in both auditory and bodily ways. Sound has the power to become an entire energetic experience

In Balance: When the Throat chakra is in balance, people will feel energetically empowered to speak their truth. An open throat chakra allows for honest and confident communication. The words coming out will be powerful, enlightened, authentic, and directed. People will be able to pour their truths upon the world like honey, liberating themselves in the process.

Out of Balance: Throat chakra imbalance may manifest psychologically as lying, being overly secretive, or living in extreme fear. It manifests physically as chronic sore throat, voice hoarseness, or other mouth or dental issues. Neck pain is, and headaches are another common symptom of imbalance, along with jaw disorders. Emotionally, an imbalanced throat chakra can elicit a general fear of speaking out and self-expression. It can lead to untrustworthiness and telling other people's secrets, as well as the inability to listen to other people. It is not uncommon to see a decrease in social skills and creativity and an increase in anxiety and detachment from other people.

Heart Chakra
Color: Green

72

Location: Chest center

Basic Description: Also known by the Sanskrit name "Anahata" (unstruck), the heart chakra is the center of compassion, beauty, and the transformative experience of love. This chakra seeks connection in the form of giving and receiving love to others and opening oneself in love. It relates to the human capacity to love, the transcendence of personal identity into true connection, perceptions of beauty, and the experience of meaningful relationships. This chakra is tied to the cardiac and respiratory systems, as well as to the immune system through its association with the thymus gland.

In Balance: When the Heart chakra is balanced, there will be an increase of empathy in people's relationships as they are able to truly relate to those around them and hold compassionate space for them. A balanced Heart chakra leads to increased self-love, self-acceptance, and self-forgiveness, which therefore makes it easier to offer these same gifts to others. True peace can be achieved through an increased ability to process grief and heal the places where the heart has hardened or broken in the past. Additionally, the sense of harmonious connection to other beings and the world will deepen.

Out of Balance: Psychologically, an imbalanced heart chakra may manifest as extreme jealousy, resistance to intimacy with others, isolation, a savior complex, or unhealthy codependency. On a physical level, imbalanced heart chakras may cause issues with the heart and circulatory system, or increase risks for respiratory diseases such as bronchitis and pneumonia. Emotionally, a person with an imbalanced Heart chakra will have a much harder time forgiving themselves and others. They will also be more likely to put up walls and practice potentially harmful defense mechanisms and will be quick to shut down and fall into the role of the victim.

Solar Plexus Chakra
Color: Yellow

Location: Stomach/abdomen

Basic Description: Also called by the Sanskrit name "Manipura" ("city of jewels"), the Solar Plexus chakra is known as the energy center which embodies the most personal power. This center is all about personal abilities, willpower, and powerful assertion within the world. This chakra relates to the prospect of taking responsibility and control over one's own life and destiny with clarity, confidence, self-discipline, intellect, and self-awareness. This chakra is known for its expression of life purpose and larger plans.

In Balance: When the Solar Plexus Chakra is balanced, people will be more assertive in achieving the results they want and need. Their orientation in the world will be harmonious, and they will be able to maintain the energy necessary to get where they want to go.

Out of Balance: Imbalances in the Solar Plexus chakra can manifest psychologically as control issues, obsessive disorders, and the tendency to become manipulative over other people. Emotionally, imbalance of the Solar Plexus chakra may cause feelings of helplessness and lack of a clear life purpose. It can also lead to a lack of follow through on tasks, plans, and relationships.

Sacral Chakra
Color: Orange

Location: Below the navel

Basic Description: Commonly called by the Sanskrit name 'Svadhisthana" ("your own place"), the Sacral chakra is tied to the emotions, body, sensuality, and sense of playful creativity and fantasy. It plays an important role in sensations, the emotional experience, and the ability for people to truly be present in both their inner and outer worlds. This chakra plays an important role in relationship building and has a special role to play when it comes to sensuality, pleasure, and sexuality. The primary motivation of this chakra is pleasure, and pleasurable experiences are what motivate a general sense of well-being and openness to the world. This chakra connects to the genital areas, as well as the lymphatic system.

In Balance: A balanced Sacral chakra creates a harmonious and pleasurable state of being in relation to other people and the world. This relationship is centered around nurturing others and sharing pleasure with them, and it allows for human beings to expand and create their identities.

Out of Balance: Psychologically, an out of balance Sacral chakra can lead to emotional numbness and deep disconnection with oneself and their emotional experience. Dependency and addictive behaviors are common due to the desire to access pleasure. Physically, imbalance in the Sacral chakra can cause a lack of sexual desire, dissatisfaction, or sexual dysfunction. On an emotional level, an imbalanced Sacral chakra can lead a person to be overcome by their emotions to a point that is not functional. They may become stuck in particular emotional states and have a very hard time moving past them.

Root Chakra

Color: Red

Location: Base of the spine

Basic Description: Sometimes called by the Sanskrit name "Muladhara" ("foundation"), the Root chakra is associated with grounding and laying a foundation for the rest of a person's life. It is tied to feelings of security, self-preservation, meeting basic needs, and being physically present in the body. The Root chakra grounds people to the earth and helps to channel their energy into practical and self-preserving ways that aid survival and safety.

In Balance: The Root chakra is the space on which people begin to construct their lives. When it is balanced, it provides constant growth, positive orientation in the world, and feeling safe enough to explore all life has to offer.

Out of Balance: Psychologically, an imbalanced Root chakra may lead to disordered eating, cynicism, and living in a constant state of fight or flight mode. People with imbalanced Root chakras are likely to suffer from severe anxiety over the idea that they can never be fully secure. Emotionally, a person with an imbalanced Root chakra is likely to be more negative, insecure with themselves in the world around them, greedy, and covetous. People with imbalanced Root chakras likely feel far more threatened in the world and may have trouble being able to obtain feelings of peace and safety.

Chapter 5: Bringing Yourself into Balance

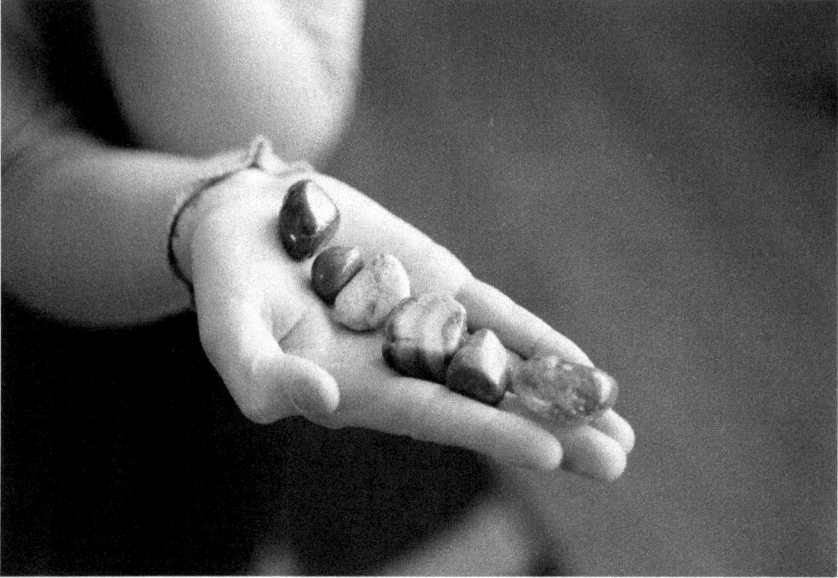

Crystals and Corresponding Chakras

The healing power of crystals has been harnessed for centuries to strengthen and balance the chakras. If you need a place to start, here is a guide of which crystals pair well with each chakra and why.

Root Chakra: If your root chakra is out of balance, you will likely be struggling with a lack of stability, feelings of insecurity, very limited willpower, and a general inability to become grounded. **Smoky quartz** has strong balancing properties that can be used to harness energy and increase protection and grounding. **Zircon** increases balance, as well as the ability to sustain it and reach high levels of purity and unity with all that is.

Hematite is another great stone for balancing the Root chakra and becoming grounded because it balances yin/yang. **Black Obsidian** also helps with grounding, as well as increasing levels of security and aiding in a person's ability to be introspective. **Black Tourmaline** is a stone that helps ward off negativity and increases vitality. Garnet is another energy-increasing stone, which also aids in the establishment of stronger willpower, devotion, and commitment to obtaining balance and getting things done. **Red Zincite** is one of the rarest stones which aligns with the Root chakra, and it aids in the establishment of personal power and creativity. This stone is also very effective at removing energy blockages and rejuvenating the body.

Sacral Chakra: If the Sacral Chakra is out of balance, people may experience a lack of creativity, reduced sexual desire and satisfaction, infertility, extreme disconnection from intuition and emotionality, and a general sense of unwellness. **Vanadinite** is a stone that allows people to enter an elevated mental state, such as in meditation, wherein a person can reach a deeper understanding and restore a sense of order to their life. *Tourmaline* can be utilized in both blue and green forms to balance the sacral chakra. **Green Tourmaline** aids creative processes, life abundance, and the healing process. **Blue Tourmaline** facilitates effective communication and increased life awareness. **Carnelian** can be used to bring things back into balance by increasing perception and warding off negativity in daily life. **Imperial Topaz** is another option for balancing the Sacral Chakra, as it promotes deep creativity, the freedom of self-expression, and the restoration of energy and love. **Orange Calcite** is a stone with properties that can open and clear out all chakra centers, allowing for increased energy and overall healing.

Solar Plexus Chakra: When the Solar Plexus Chakra is imbalanced, people are likely to be lethargic, uninspired, lacking ambition, and generally lacking a sense of personal power. **Gold Tiger Eye** works to restore optimism, awareness, and life balance. **Golden Calcite** is a stone that can be used to drastically increase energy levels and corresponding ambition. **Yellow Apatite** works to stimulate the self-realization necessary for change. **Citrine** is one of the most powerful stones for clearing negative energies, building endurance, promoting enthusiasm, and expanding levels of self-esteem and life abundance.

Heart Chakra: When the heart chakra is out of balance, people will struggle more with being compassionate and extending love towards others. They may lack the ability to balance emotions and may also be far removed from consciousness. There are three types of Tourmaline that aid in balancing the Heart Chakra. The first is **Rubellite (dark pink) Tourmaline,** which restores creativity and loving devotion. **Pink Tourmaline** also aids in love, as well as increased understanding, spirituality, sense of calm, and capacity for joy. **Watermelon Tourmaline** works similarly as it specifically activates the energy of the Heart Chakra and helps clear blockages. **Lepidolite** restores honesty and helps create feelings of hope in the midst of life challenges and relationship difficulties. **Green Aventurine** aids in the balance of male and female energies, which can be incredibly helpful in creating balance in relationships. **Pink Danburite** is a purifying stone that aids in the removal of toxins from the body and helps restore communication and relationship building. **Malachite** is a necessary stone for the power of transformation, which is required to fully balance the Heart Chakra. This stone helps people grow in understanding and compassion of their own body and life experience and increases personal power and intuition. It may lead people to become more aware of how emotions are manifested physically in their bodies and take responsibility to make the changes needed. **Rose Quartz**, the stone of love itself, is the most powerful stone for balancing the Heart Chakra. This stone helps replace negative energy in relationships with positive energy, emotional harmony, compassion, and sexual balance. This stone also aids in forgiveness of the past and helps release negative emotions that are stored (like anger, fear, and jealousy).

Throat Chakra: If the Throat Chakra is imbalanced, people will face greater barriers to communication and self-expression, and are likely to lack a strong sense of purpose. **Aquamarine** is known for inspiring the courage necessary to look inside oneself and become truly aware of the areas which are lacking. **Celestite** is helpful in developing communication skills, fostering harmony, and clearing the mind. **Chrysocolla** aids communication as well by providing people with a more profound inner strength. **Amazonite** can be used to soothe a person into a place where they feel safer to open up and can more easily become attuned to spirituality. **Blue Kyanite** is useful for fostering the mental awareness necessary for effective communication. **Sodalite** aids in truth-telling. **Blue Chalcedony** helps balance energies of the body, mind, and spirit, and is widely used for improving group dynamics and kind, harmonious communication.

Third Eye Chakra: When the Third Eye Chakra is out of balance, people are likely to lack spiritual attunement and intuition. As the "Stone of Heaven," **Azurite** is known for stimulating the Third Eye in deeper intuition, sense of Enlightenment, and even psychic abilities. **Tanzanite** is a stone which yields cohesivity of personal power, psychic power, and the spiritual realm. Additionally, this stone can be a source of guidance on a person's journey to self-actualization.

Crown Chakra: Imbalanced Crown Chakras produce difficulty in obtaining higher consciousness. **Selenite** grants the mental clarity necessary to gain deeper insight and awareness, sometimes even into past and future lives. **White Topaz** is useful in stimulating energy, a sense of individuality, and thought patterns and loving actions that lead people towards their highest selves. **White Howlite** can serve to eliminate the negative emotions of stress, anger, and physical or emotional pain, while also increasing discernment and personal progress. **White Danburite** helps with increased intellectualism. **Amethyst** has the ability to abolish illusions about the world and aid in channeling abilities. This stone is known for producing greater peace, contentment, and personal strength. As the "Crystal of Attunement," the **Herkimer Diamond** can develop a sense of harmony, awareness, and a deeper connection to all that is. **Apophyllite** is the stone that bridges the gap between the physical and spiritual realms, facilitating astral travel, future gazing, and a sense of universal love and purity.

Plants, Herbs, Oils, and Corresponding Chakras

Root Chakra: The Root Chakra is responsible for keeping us grounded not only to the physical earth but also in the present moment. **_Dandelion root_** can be used to treat out of balance Root Chakras and work to heal depression, autoimmune diseases, low immunity, and pain in the lower parts of the body (legs, feet, tailbone, etc.) Consuming **_root vegetables_**, such as garlic, onions, carrots, and potatoes, can also be healing to the Root Chakra.

Sacral Chakra: When the Sacral Chakra is out of balance, the aromatic **_gardenia_** can be used for its roots or oil to restore creativity and happiness. There are a number of **_herbs and spices_** which aid in restoring the Sacral Chakra to full creativity, sensuality, and self-expression, including cinnamon, vanilla, Coriander, licorice, and fennel. **_Sandalwood_** can be applied to the body in oil form or burned in herb form to unblock the Sacral Chakra and aid in fertility, recovery from disordered eating, curing infection, protecting the urinary tract, and overcoming emotional imbalances.

Solar Plexus Chakra: Several **_herbs and spices_** used to facilitate emotional wellbeing and self-control include: peppermint, ginger, Lily of the valley, cinnamon, turmeric, and cumin. **_Bergamot_** can be used (most commonly in oil form) to aid in digestive health.

Lavender oil can be used on the body or diffused in the air or a bath to bring people out of depressed, anxious, or untrusting states of being into a state of calm mental and bodily relaxation. This is incredibly important, because poor mental health, self-doubt, and feelings of unworthiness can lead to digestive issues, liver and kidney issues, eating disorders, and ulcers. *Rosemary* is used in oil or herb form to calm the stomach and restore intestinal health.

Heart Chakra: **Hawthorne berries** in a tincture or a tea are one of the best herbal remedies for healing the heart chakra from grief, anger, jealousy, loneliness, hatred, and difficulty loving ourselves and others. By resolving these emotional issues, our sense of empathy, spiritual devotion, and physical hearth health and circulation can be restored. Several other useful *oils and herbs* for balancing the Heart Chakra are: rose, lavender, thyme, basil, jasmine, sage, cilantro, and Cayenne.

Throat Chakra: The issues with self-expression and difficulty communicating that arise with a blocked Throat Chakra can be aided by the use of **red clover blossom**, typically in the form of a tea. Healing of the Throat Chakra also aids in protection or recovery from issues with emotional codependence, spiritual insecurity, chronic fear, and anxiety, as well as physical issues with the thyroid or laryngitis. **Lemon balm** and **eucalyptus oil** applied topically to the chest are useful for thyroid health and throat decongestion. Several helpful **herbs and spices** for the throat chakra are lemongrass, sage, salt, and peppermint.

Third-Eye Chakra: **Mint** is a useful herb for healing depression by facilitating a deeper connection between the mind, body, and universe as a whole. It is also used to treat chronic migraines and improve memory and vigilance. **Eyebright** is an herb used to bring understanding of the "lights and darks" of life, produce a sense of mental clarity, and improve physical eye health. Juniper, jasmine, lavender, rosemary, and poppy seed are all useful **herbs and oils** for restoring imagination, intuition, and better sleep.

Crown Chakra: **Lotus flowers** are known to enhance a sense of divine wisdom and interconnectedness and restore a sense of universal connection in healing the Crown Chakra. **Lavender flowers** are also useful for enhancing meditation, bringing the soul into alignment, restring spiritual connection, and a sense of cosmic love. Teas, baths, aromatherapy, and some Japanese and Chinese dishes, are excellent ways to incorporate these flowers for healing.

Chakra Balancing Activities

Root Chakra: In order to balance the Root Chakra, your focus should be on grounding and coming back to connection with the earth. This can happen through any **outdoor activity.** Whether it's going for a hike, taking a walk, or simply finding a place in nature to sit, time in nature is crucial for bringing the Root Chakra into balance. **Grounding** is another effective practice for balancing the Root Chakra. This simply involves standing in the grass or soil with bare feet, preferably for a minimum of thirty minutes. In this time, the body can become saturated with the energies of the earth and fall back into balance with the rhythm of nature. If you can find at least fifteen minutes a day to stand with your bare feet on the earth, you are sure to notice a deeper sense of balance and presence in your environment.

Sacral Chakra: **Self-care practices** are vital for balancing the Sacral Chakra. This can come in the form of pampering oneself with a massage or a facial, taking a relaxing bubble bath, settling down with your favorite beverage and a good book, etc. Whatever self-care looks like for you, your Sacral Chakra needs it. Allowing yourself to **become aware of your emotions** through journaling, art, listening to music, or watching a movie that stirs your emotions, is another important element to balancing the sacral chakra. **Dancing** is another excellent way to channel this emotional energy, especially improvisational/lyrical dance, which focuses on free-flowing movements. Another tip for balancing the Sacral Chakra is to **imagine yourself as a body of water**, whether this be in meditation while dancing or creating, or while swimming and becoming a part of the body of water you're emerged in.

Solar Plexus Chakra: **Exercise** is one of the best ways to balance the Solar Plexus chakra. This may be swimming, going for a run, going to the gym, or simply doing a few yoga poses or sit-ups. **Spending time in the sun** in the hours of the early morning (before 10 a.m.) or the evening (after 4 p.m.) is another great option for balancing the Solar Plexus Chakra and recharging your life center. Another great option for stimulating your life center and balancing the energies of the Solar Plexus Chakra is in **trying a new activity or visiting a new place.**

Heart Chakra: **Random acts of kindness/love** are the best way to restore and balance your Heart Chakra. Doing kind things for other people helps your heart to soften, open, and generate loving energy in the world. **Connecting deeply with other people** through shared smiles, eye contact, and intense "heart-to-heart" conversations are another excellent way to get energy flowing in your Heart Chakra. Another way to restore balance, especially when the Heart Chakra feels particularly hardened, tense, angry, or emotionally blocked off, is to come back to the moment with **deep breathing**. Breathe love in, and exhale anxiety, anger, hatred, fear.

Throat Chakra: **Writing** is a great way to put your truth into words, coming to terms with your own voice and experience and restoring the balance and self-expression to the Throat Chakra. If you find yourself struggling to share your truth verbally, writing is one of the best ways to get you back to that space. When you are ready, another way to balance the Throat Chakra is by allowing yourself to **share your voice** in conversations, not holding back on your thoughts and feelings. Remind yourself as many times as you need to that what you have to say is valid and worth being embraced.

Third-Eye Chakra: Your intuition and feelings of deeper purpose are achieved by **turning inward**. **Visualization practices** are crucial for restoring balance to the Third Eye Chakra. This may look like imagining yourself reaching your goals, achieving what you dream of, or being in a scenario where you are entirely at peace. This can also be allowing yourself to **imagine your highest self**. How does your highest self orient in the world? What is important to them? Which elements of their personality are most prominent? What is their lifestyle?

Crown Chakra: **Meditation** is the key to a balanced Crown Chakra. It is important to find some way to meditate every single day, even if it is only for 1-5 minutes. It is during this time that you can cultivate the silence, awareness, and openness that is required to feel fully in touch with your highest self. Allow yourself *quiet time* every day, **without distraction**, to have this experience.

Chapter 6: Chakra Check-In

Daily Energy Check-in to Monitor your Chakras

The following practice is derived from the energy healing practice of *reiki*, which involves restoring balance to each of the body's energy centers through touch/hands-on healing. While most reiki practice requires certification, this technique is one that you can do on yourself daily without any formal training.

In this practice, you will be laying your hands on various parts of your body. Begin by washing your hands; you may apply a lightly-scented lotion or essential oil if it is pleasing to you.

Position 1- Hands Over Eyes: Place the palms of your hands over your eye sockets, with your fingers stretched up towards the top of your head. Press lightly, holding for at least one minute. You may switch the position of your hands to have your fingers pointing inwards towards your nose, or outwards in a triangular shape to the sides of your head. Regardless of which position you choose, allow yourself to feel the movement of your eyes. Relax your face, letting all tension fall away. Take notice of any sensations. One minute is the minimum amount of time to hold, but you may hold as long as you want until you feel warmth in the area, and energy is freely flowing.

Position 2- Hands Over Ears: Cup your ears in your palms, gently clasping the back of your skull with your fingertips. You may massage lightly around the ears to ease any tension and drain lymphatic fluid. Remain here for at least one minute, holding as long as you need to feel the tension melt away and feel an increase of warm energy.

Position 3- Hands Over Temples: Move your hands to the sides of your head, clasping your thumbs underneath your jawbone. Press lightly into your temples, taking notice of any tingling, throbbing, or other sensations. Remain for at least one minute, or until you begin to feel the warmth or tingle of energy flow.

Position 4- Hands Over Whole Head: Place one hand horizontally across your forehead, clasping the crown of your head with the other hand. Press slightly harder, allowing yourself to come into the moment and feeling all distractions in your mind give way to clarity. This is one of the most grounding reiki positions, and you can use it on its own to center yourself throughout the day.

Position 5- Hands Over Throat: Clasp your hands around your throat in a crossed position (one over the other). Imagine your throat opening and your truth flowing freely from it. Take notice of any sensations you feel. You may also move your fingers to the side of your neck, keeping your palms centered, and begin to gently massage lymphatic fluid downwards towards the heart.

Position 6- Hands Over Heart: Position your fingertips towards the center of the chest, with your palms pressing just slightly above the nipple line. Feel the warmth and energy flowing into your chest, pulling slightly to the sides in an effort to "open" the heart. You may switch positions, moving your fingertips to face the navel. Hold for at least one minute, observing any sensation that arises as your heart opens.

Position 7- Hands Over Abdomen: Place your hands about midway down your torso, slightly above your navel. Point your fingertips inwards towards each other. Hold yourself securely, imagining restoration of your life force. Feel any weightiness or other sensations that arise in your stomach area. Hold for at least one minute.

Position 8- Hands Over Sacrum: Angle your fingertips down slightly, creating a triangular shape around your hips/lower abdomen. Notice any sensations of tingling, arousal, etc. that arise. Hold the energy here for at least one minute, warming and opening.

Position 9- Hands Over Thighs: To balance the Root Chakra, place your palms on the tops of your thighs, fingertips pointing downwards. Hold for at least one minute, allowing yourself to feel grounded up through your spine and down through the soles of your feet.

Chakra Check-In Daily Meditation With Journaling (Week 4)

After completing your basic chakra check-in, grab a pen and some paper and write out each of the seven chakras with some space next to it (Crown, Third Eye, Throat, Heart, Solar Plexus, Sacral, Root)

Consider each chakra, one by one, with the question, "What do I observe in my *particular chakra* today?"

Write down your levels of balance and any feelings you have about the energy in each chakra

Consider the chakras which feel most out of balance and ask yourself, "What am I going to integrate into my life today to re-balance these chakras?" Write your ideas down.

PART IV

Chapter 1: Energy Healing- The Key to Holistic Health

Understanding the impacts of energy imbalances and corresponding physical, mental, spiritual health

How many times have you, or another adult in your life, said the words "I just don't have the energy I used to have."? Most adults know the feeling of looking at the energy children have as they run about, enjoying life, exploring their surroundings, and never seeming to grow tired. Many of us are left reflecting back on the distant past when we, too, had such energy and wondering where it went.

From the time children enter school, they begin to be presented with expectations. Stand in a straight line, raise your hand, don't talk while the teacher is talking. Each year, the level of responsibility and expectation seems to increase. While rules, regulations, and individual responsibility are important for a functioning society, there are numerous expectations and social pressures put on people as they grow, which can be incredibly harmful.

It is generally around middle school when children become more acutely aware of their bodies and societal beauty standards, which tell them what they "should" look like. Children are likely to become aware of the trends, such as which clothes the "cool kids" are wearing. The endless battle to feel like enough begins, and can lead to a plethora of issues with self-esteem, eating disorders, and mental illness. In addition to the basic societal pressures to be accepted and considered attractive, many children are also faced with difficult situations at home where their own needs are not being met, they are having to provide for and protect themselves in the only ways they know how, avoid abusive parents, care for younger siblings, or worry about if they'll have anything to eat that day. Even if children have a relatively healthy home life, this is the age when they will begin to become aware of the issues that plague their family (every family has issues) whether this is divorce, an alcoholic parent, the death of a pet or loved one, etc.

We live in a society that thrives off of consumerism. We are flooded with images of how the next vacation, new pair of shoes, nicer car, nicer house, or perfect partner will make us happy, and all of the things we need to change about ourselves in order to fulfill those things. Eventually, all the energy we had as a child starts going towards maintaining our image in society, trying to have all the "best" life has to offer (which always happens to be everything we do not have), and attempting to be as "successful" as possible in the eyes of society and other people. With no time to rest in the present moment, recharge, and appreciate what we already have, it is no wonder, so many of us are completely drained of energy. In such a fast-paced society that discourages breaks, our energy will become depleted, and we will find ourselves thrown out of balance and unable to obtain true happiness and well-being. Over time, this depletion and imbalance can lead to a sense of spiritual disconnection, extreme mental health issues, and an increased risk of physical pain, illness, and even earlier death.

Chapter 2: Energy Healing and Overcoming Suffering

Energy and Grief/Trauma

Every human being knows that loss is a natural part of life. The one certain thing in life is that we, and everyone we know, is going to die. However, in such a fast-paced society, we are often given a very short grace period before being expected to swallow our grief and "move on" when we lose those closest to us. It is not abnormal for people to receive a bereavement period of only a few days before being expected to be back in the classroom or office and be fully functional. There is very little space for the grief journey, and most people are expected to harbor their feelings and keep their grief to themselves.

The grief process is expansive and incredibly energy draining. When we don't receive the adequate support from those around us, or adequate space to heal, our body begins to break down piece by piece. The empty spaces within us will swallow us up into states of depression, numbness, isolation, and pure exhaustion. Just like a wound being denied the correct treatment and care, the wounds of unresolved grief will fester and leave us feeling completely drained of energy and vitality for life.

Unresolved trauma also has an incredibly destructive impact on the body. Trauma can occur as a result of grief itself, as well as emotional or domestic abuse, accident or illness, war, sexual assault, childhood maltreatment, etc. The body holds trauma in various places, and the brain switches over from the logical ability to discern safety and danger into an easily triggered emotional state. An overactive emotional brain loses the ability to think clearly, make decisions, and recognize threats. People who have unresolved trauma are likely to be easily triggered and deal with unexplained outbursts of anger, fear, relationship issues, reckless behavior, and health problems. When trauma sits in the body unresolved, the brain is unable to understand that the traumatic event has ended. Therefore, it will stay in a consistent fight-or-flight state, which is incredibly draining and will leave the body with no energy. Not only will trauma victims experience low energy levels, but they will also experience severe issues maintaining positive relationships and overall well-being.

Energy and Mental Health

There are numerous factors that can contribute to mental health issues. As previously discussed, societal issues and unresolved grief and trauma can yield higher levels of anxiety, depression, and PTSD. It is also very common for people to suffer from mood disorders, personality disorders, disordered eating, substance abuse, etc. The list is long for psychological ailments and how they happen, and it has been proven that 1 in 3 people will be diagnosed with a mental illness in their lifetime. Even without a specific disorder, most people will have periods of life where their mental health suffers greatly.

No matter what a person's struggle with mental health looks like, or what they are doing (or not doing) in terms of treatment, the body expends a lot of energy when a part of it is unwell.

Daily Energy Regulation

No matter what it is in your life that is causing you to feel depleted, it is vital to pay attention to the energy fields within the body and identify the areas of greatest pain and imbalance. In the spectrum of health, people often take measures such as going to see the doctor, therapist, or grief counselor, taking medication, and making lifestyle changes such as finding a hobby or increasing exercise. However, a piece that is commonly overlooked in the healing journey is healing energetically. No matter how much you invest in your mental, physical, emotional, and spiritual health, if your energies remain imbalanced, it is impossible to reach a state of full wellness. That being said, energy healing is the missing piece in most people's quests for holistic health.

In many cases, it can be beneficial to seek the help of energy healers, massage therapists, and reiki, craniosacral therapy, or bodywork practitioners. These practitioners are trained in getting in touch with your energy centers and helping bring them back into balance through healing touch, body movements, and visualization techniques. If you are dealing with energy imbalance, seeing a practitioner can be an excellent investment in unlocking your highest levels of health and joy in life.

It is also possible to use a variation of the body scan mediation from chapter 3 to check in with your energy levels on your own. By taking notice of the sensations in each area of your body, you can come closer in touch with any area of your body where you experience regular pain, tension, or other unpleasant feelings. This is often a sign of imbalance or trapped energy. Additionally, the tense and release technique in each area of the body can yield healing and balance by releasing negative energy and tension. It is important to check in with yourself daily, asking your body where energy may be trapped or depleted and what you can do to replenish yourself.

Chapter 3: The Daily Energy Healing Journey

Understanding Your Energy Field: Daily Energy Healing Meditation with Journaling (Week 5)

There is a great variety when it comes to human energy fields. People experience varying levels of sensitivity to the energy of other people and the environment. Some people are incredibly in tune with "vibes"; others are empaths who feel the emotional experiences of others on a deep level, while still others experience very little of either. There is also a lot of variation in the way people recharge energetically, as well as what depletes them. In the common case of introverts and extroverts, for example, introverts need time alone to replenish their energy and feel balanced, while extroverts recharge in stimulating environments with other people around. One of the first steps to protecting your personal energetic field is to understand how it works.

Understanding Your Energy Field Journal Prompt (Week 5):

When you feel exhausted and not like yourself, which activities are most likely to replenish your energy? Do you enjoy a night out with friends? Yoga? A walk in the park? Leisure reading? Finding a new adventure? Taking a bubble bath? Listening to your favorite music on blast? List 5-10 activities that help you gain balance and feel energized.

Now, make a list of the things that make you feel most drained. These can be large things, like a specific task at your job, or small things like doing the dishes. You may find that you feel drained if you spend too much time alone or, consequently, when you spend too much time around other people.

When it comes to activities that make you feel drained, ask yourself to what extent that specific thing is necessary in your life. If you find yourself feeling drained from spending too much time around other people, for example, you can easily make a change by scheduling more "nothing time" or "alone time" into your days and taking the time you need to replenish. Household tasks and daily responsibilities are necessary, but by being aware of the ones that drain you the most, you can bring more attention to the process and doing what you need to replenish energy before or after.

Protecting Your Energy Field: Daily Energy Healing Meditation with Journaling (Week 6)

Close your eyes and ask yourself, "what does my energy field look like?" Write down any specific colors, textures, shapes, or patterns of movement.

Once you have an image in your mind of your energy field, ask yourself, "What does it look like for outside energies to enter my field?" Write down what healthy and unhealthy outside energies look like.

Then ask yourself, "How can I regulate the energies entering my field? What does it look like when I decide what I will let in?" Describe this process.

Finally, ask yourself, "How does my body feel when I regulate what I allow to enter my energy field?" Write down everything that comes to mind.

Healing Through Trapped Emotion Release: Daily Energy Healing Meditation with Journaling (Week 7)

In our society, we are often faced with life circumstances that force us to repress our basic human emotions. It is very possible for anger, rage, or grief to become stuck in the body because it is considered "impractical" to have those reactions in public. Similarly, we often hear about people being described as "annoyingly happy" or "overly emotional." Most of us are taught not only to manage our emotions but to distance ourselves from them and react emotionally only in certain contexts. Additionally, we tend to suppress negative emotions such as fear, shame, inadequacy, and insecurity, for the purpose of appearing like we have everything together. Between life events and societal expectations, it is very easy for the emotions we suppress to become trapped in our bodies, which can create adverse health effects, negatively impact our relationships, and keep us from living our best lives.

Begin by making a list of as many emotions as you can think of

Run down the list of emotions one by one, asking yourself, "Is there anywhere in my body I am holding *particular emotion*?"

Write down the emotions you feel are trapped. Take some time to journal about how certain emotions arose, or times when you felt you had to suppress your emotions.

With each emotion you have labeled as being trapped, write: "I give myself permission to release this *particular emotion*

Cultivating Self-Trust in your Healing Journey: Daily Energy Healing Meditation With Journaling (Week 8)

No matter what you do in your life, there will always be people who don't understand the choices you make, or who judge the path you are on. When it comes to renewing and protecting your energy, there is no room for anyone else's opinions or emotions in regards to your journey. It requires a great deal of self-trust to go your own way and let what other people think about it roll off your back. For this reason, it is vital to begin everyday establishing a sense of self-trust with your own journey and energy management skills. The following four journal questions will help you direct your energy before going about your day.

What are you most grateful for today?

What are your intentions for how you will direct your energy today?

What are your fears/things you perceive as a potential threat?

What are your commitments to yourself and the world?

Mini Meditation Toolbox: 25 Quick and Easy Energy Restoration and
Protection Meditations

One-Minute Energy Cleanse

- This meditation is useful if you find yourself with a person or in a specific situation that feels negative or energetically draining. You do not need to be alone to complete this meditation

- Pause where you are and allow yourself to take a few deep, cleansing breaths

- Focus exclusively on your breathing; you may close your eyes or leave them open

- Feel the inner power within the core of your body, around your abdomen. Remind yourself that you are in control and have the power to maintain balance.

- As you inhale, pull love, light, and peace into your body

- As you exhale, breathe out pain, annoyance, and toxicity

Energy from the Earth

- Begin by entering a space in nature. This can be on the beach, in the mountains, near a river, in a garden, by the lake, or in your own yard

- If possible, slip your shoes off, so your bare feet are in contact with the earth

- Start with a few cleansing breaths, taking note of everything you see, hear, smell, and feel in your environment

- Placing the soles of your feet on the ground, begin to breathe, pulling the energy from the earth up through your body

- Remember that you are One with the nature that courses around you. Allow it to heal what is broken within you and leave you feeling rejuvenated

Re-Centering Head Hold (3-5 minute meditation)

- Close your eyes and place the palm of one hand horizontally across the crown of your head, and the other palm across your forehead (over the energetic points of the Crown and Third Eye chakras). This position can be done while standing, sitting, or lying down.

- While clutching your head in this position, bring attention to any sensations in your body. What needs your attention most right now?

- Allow yourself to come back to the present moment, feeling grounded in your body and in your experience

- Breathe in awareness, focus, and comfort, exhaling anxiety and distraction

- When you open your eyes, notice how you feel grounded in your space

The Cloak of Protection

- This meditation is useful for energy protection before going out into the world, whether that is to work, the supermarket, an appointment, etc.

- Although you do not know what kinds of energies you may encounter, or which people may try to take your energy from you, remind yourself that you are in control of your own energy and that you have the capacity to protect yourself

- Close your eyes and imagine a dark-blue, almost black cloak made of a soft, thick material like a velvet night sky. The cloak is full-length with a hood to protect all of your chakras.

- Imagine a ray of light outlining the cloak in whatever color(s) feel most magical, protective, and authentic to who you are

- Set off into the world knowing that you are safe within yourself and your energy cloak and that you do not need to be afraid

De-Cluttering your Space

- When energy is lacking or out of balance, the spaces we live in are likely to reflect that imbalance with clutter and messiness. The more we feel like we "don't have our lives together," the more likely we are to have a messy desk, dishes piling up in the sink, laundry that still needs to be folded, or a car that has not been cleared of trash

- Such spaces do not allow for peace and mental clarity and can be even more draining to come back to after a long day

- Dedicate yourself to one area of your life to de-clutter. This can be your kitchen, your car, your bedroom, etc. Close your eyes before beginning and take a few deep, cleansing breaths to approach the task calmly

- Begin to address all of the clutter in the space, not only picking it up but putting it into a designated area where it can be organized and easy to find

- You may find that you want to create a special shelf or move some furniture around to make the space less cluttered. As you go, notice the energy that continues to unfold in your body

- When you finish, place a "clutter basket" in your room, the car, the living room, etc. where you can compile all the clutter throughout the day and put it away before bed

De-Cluttering your Mind (5-minute meditation)

- Close your eyes and begin to breathe deeply

- Ask yourself, "What is taking up the most space in my mind right now?"

- Bring your attention to whatever it is that is distracting you, and why it makes you feel out of control

- Breathe into that situation, saying, "I have control over this situation, and I am not going to let it spill out into the rest of my day. I am clearing this space."

The Energy-Ownership Mantra

- This meditation is ideal to perform in the morning, or before going out to interact with the world or other people

- Sit in a place where you feel energized (on the porch, in your meditation corner, etc.)

- Close your eyes and begin to breathe, checking in with any unresolved emotions or senses within the body

- Now begin to picture your energy field. Say to yourself: "My energy field is my sacred space, and other energies will only permeate it when I allow them to."

- Breathe into this thought for several moments

- Now, bring this thought into your mental space: "I have the wisdom to discern what belongs to me and what belongs to other people. I can be empathetic and attentive to other people's emotions, struggles, and opinions without assuming responsibility for them."

Epsom Bath Energy Renewal

- Begin by selecting your favorite scented Epsom salts. You may also customize your bath with petals, oils, and candles as according to the healing plants, herbs, and oils listed in Chapter 4

- Run a hot bath, letting your Epsom salts and other elements saturate the water

- Customize your space with the light of candles, meditative music, and anything else that makes you feel at peace

- Find a comfortable position inside the tub. Close your eyes, and feel your entire body relax into the heat and gentle movement of the water.

- Begin to conduct a body scan, feeling entirely vulnerable to this moment at peace with only yourself

- Ask your body, "What do I need right now?"

- The water should be hot enough that you begin to sweat (be sure to have a glass of water nearby). As you sweat, imagine your body purging itself of every blockage, every impurity, and every negativity

Sealing your Energy Field

- Close your eyes and begin to breathe

- Bring the image of your energy field to your mind. You may picture a wall, a bubble, or a glowing ring of light (this image may also differ depending on the day)

- Picture what other energies look like, floating around your field like particles in an atom. Say to yourself, "I am in control of what comes in."

- Imagine yourself recognizing people who are trying to take your energy or bear their burdens. Imagine any fear, anger, or resentment you may feel.

- Say to yourself, "No, not today." Imagine your bubble becoming impermeable, your wall being sealed, your glowing ring of light rejecting anything that does not belong inside
- Allow yourself to feel empowered over your energy, without feeling any resentment or judgment towards those who once posed a threat

Building your Sanctuary

- Sit down and close your eyes, beginning to breathe into yourself
- With each breath, ask yourself, "What makes me feel safe?" Repeat three times.
- Switch the phrase to "What makes me feel at peace?" Repeat three times.
- Switch the phrase to "What makes me feel loving?" Repeat three times
- Switch to "What makes me feel joy?"
- Lastly, ask yourself, "What makes me feel renewed?"
- When you ask yourself these questions, you may see certain crystals, scenes in nature, types of music, plants, aromas, decorations, activities, or color schemes. Take note of whatever comes to mind.
- Use these things that come to you in meditation to mindfully cultivate a space for yourself to come into every day when you need time to recharge. This can be a meditation corner, a spot in the

backyard, or any other space that is sacred to you and provides feelings of security and rest.

Cultivating Non-Reaction

- This meditation can be used when encountering a stressful situation, having a difficult conversation, or otherwise entering a state of nervous or angry energy
- Before responding to whatever the negative stimulant is, breathe into the moment. Close your eyes if needed.
- Tell yourself, "I can choose not to expend energy on this interaction. I can choose to move peacefully into the next moment."
- Feel the tension within you melt away as you make the choice not to internalize the stress of the situation or the negative energy coming at you

Boundary Setting

- Find a quiet place to sit and self-reflect. Breathe into the moment
- After you have settled into your breath, ask yourself, "What people, circumstances, or tasks drain my energy and leave me feeling agitated or exhausted?"
- Allow the answers to rise into your consciousness at will. Meditate on every name, every task, every circumstance which makes you feel tense and throws your energy out of balance.

- With each name, circumstance, and task, say to yourself, "This *person, place, thing* has no power over me. I can maintain my energy in spite of it."

- Next, ask yourself, "Where do I need to draw the line with this *person, place, thing*?"

- Listen to your intuition tell you what your boundaries should be. Perhaps, this looks like gently cutting off a toxic person, or limiting your interaction time with them. It could be quitting a job that is no longer good for you or asking for accommodations to make your environment more positive. It could be telling someone who expects you to bear their burdens that their energies are no longer your responsibility. Or, perhaps it is to establish a self-care activity to do directly after a draining task.

Trigger Awareness

- If your energy has ever been thrown out of balance by trauma, there are likely still factors of your environment that can strike at any time, causing your body to react in the same way it did at the time of the trauma.

- Breathe into the moment, asking yourself, "what elements of my environment cause me to lose control of my logic and feel afraid, helpless, irrational, in pain, or otherwise unbalanced or unhealthy energetically."

- These elements are called "triggers." Bring your awareness to these triggers, simply allowing them to be there without judgment.

- Say to yourself, "that moment in time is over. I can now release myself."

Energetic Tapping

- Begin by determining 3-5 affirmations or manifestations for the day ahead ("I manifest peace," "I am content," "I am present," "I manifest energy," "I am growing," "I manifest healing," "I manifest loving-kindness," etc.)
- Breathe deeply, pondering the affirmations/manifestations
- Choose your first manifestation/affirmation. With your index and middle fingers on both hands, begin tapping lightly on the crown of your head, repeating the manifestation or affirmation three times
- Move to the temples, tapping and saying the manifestation/affirmation three times
- Repeat at the inner corners of the brow bone
- Repeat just above the brow line
- Repeat at the top of the cheekbones
- Repeat below the ear lobes at the crest of the jawbone
- Repeat at the top of the chest
- Repeat on the left wrist, then switch to the right wrist
- Switch to the next affirmation/manifestation and go through the process again, staying in touch with your breath throughout

Listening to your Intuition

- Find a space where you feel completely comfortable and relaxed

- Begin to breathe deeply, coming into the present moment

- Ask yourself, "What does my inner self need me to know right now?"

- Keep breathing, holding space for whatever answer arises

- If necessary, you can ask follow-up questions to yourself, like "Is there any threat I need to be prepared to protect myself from?" or "How can I best love the world today?" Or "What do I need to do to take care of myself today?"

- Continue to breathe and hold space, trusting that your heart will guide you to make the correct decisions for yourself

Memory Reclamation (specifically for healing of trauma victims)

- Find a space where you feel totally safe and undisturbed. It is best to do this meditation on a day where you can invest in self-care and rest.

- Begin to breathe, telling yourself, "I am safe. I am safe. I am safe."

- Allow the memory of a particularly traumatic event to come to your mind. Continue to breathe, telling yourself, "I am safe."

- Pay attention to the details of that memory. What do you see? What do you hear? What do you feel?

- As the memory progresses, allow it to release its energetic hold on your body. Tell yourself, "That was then. This is now. I am safe."

- Feel the trauma release its hold on you, restoring itself to a basic memory of the past

Defining your Needs

- Sit in a peaceful place, breathing into the moment

- Bring attention to any pain or unrest within your body. Without judgment, allow it to be there, asking if there is anything you should learn from it.

- Generally, where there is pain or unrest, there is a need being left unmet. Ask yourself, "What is it that I need?"

- Allow your needs to arise into your consciousness ("I need a day off for my mental health," "I need a trip into nature," "I need a bath," "I need a warm, nourishing meal," "I need to go to sleep early," etc.)

- Breathe into each need, envisioning yourself meeting that particular need

- Ask yourself, "Is there anyone else I need to make aware of these needs?"

- Envision yourself having a calm conversation about your needs with your boss, your partner, your family, or a friend. Envision them, reacting gently and yourself feeling better understood and supported.

- Continue to breathe into your capacity to meet your energetic needs and make those needs known to others.

"Nothing Time"

- Set aside a minimum of one hour of time with absolutely nothing scheduled

- Sit down, breathing into the moment. Tell yourself, "this is my time. I have nowhere to be, nothing to do; I do not need to feel rushed."

- Allow your deepest intuition to guide your next step. Do whatever comes to mind first

- While you proceed with your "nothing time," allow your breath to guide every move

Discovering your Support System

- Bring your attention to the present moment, focusing on your breath

- Ask yourself, "Who of the people I know understands and embraces me for who I truly am?"

- Breathe with each name that comes up, allowing loving-kindness and appreciation for that person to flow through your body

- Ask yourself, "Who in my life encourages me to reach my full potential?

- Repeat the action of breathing with each name that arises

- Ask yourself, "Who in my life do I feel most at rest with?"

- Repeat the action of breathing with each name that arises

- Continue to breathe, saying to yourself, "These are my people. This is my support system. I will allow myself to lean on them when I need to."

Glowing Love-Energy

- Find a restful position and begin to breathe

- Imagine the aura of your energy field. How big is it? What color is it?

- Say to yourself, "I am pure love. I have room to love the entire universe and everything in it."

- Continue to repeat this phrase with every breath. Picture the aura expanding and glowing brighter

Jaguar Spirit Animal Protection

- Bring yourself into the present moment with deep breathing

- From the depth of your being, say, "I call on the spirit of the jaguar to protect me."

- Feel the reverberations of the jaguar's protection through your body, aiding you in repelling negative energy and toxicity
- Imagine a fierce, beautiful guard of your energy field, encircling you with fierce love and security

Energetic Breathing (1-3-minute meditation)

- Take some space away from your everyday life (in the bathroom, in the car, etc.) to just breathe
- Implement the 5-5-7 breathing technique
- With every breath in, say to yourself, "I breathe in pure energy."
- With every breath out, say to yourself, "I breathe out *exhaustion, *toxicity, *negativity, etc."
- Continue until you feel the tingle of pure energy coursing through your veins

Energetic Dancing/Movement

- Find a space where you can be alone and feel completely secure
- Play a song that stirs your soul and emotions, causing you to have a visceral reaction in the body each time you hear it
- As the song begins, close your eyes and deep breathe, maybe swaying back and forth slightly

- When you feel ready, release your body to move as it feels led. No choreography, no expectations, simply letting the movement of the moment lead your body into a state of pure surrender and release

- Surrender entirely to the moment, trusting your body to release any tension or trauma

- Give your body the space and freedom to heal, coming into energetic harmony

The Art of Saying "No"

- Close your eyes and begin to breathe deeply

- Begin to consider the things that drain your energy. Perhaps you have a tendency to overcommit or find yourself stuck in a relationship or circumstance that no longer serves you. Breathe with each of these places where you feel stuck

- Say to yourself "I have the power to say 'no.'"

- Imagine yourself having the necessary conversation, turning down the opportunity, or simply choosing to remove yourself from the situation

- Feel the power of saying no and being in full control of where you place your energy

The Restorative Power of Letting Go

- Breathe deeply, cultivating a sense of full peace and security

- Ask yourself, "Where are the parts of me that I need to get back?"

- Take notice of every person or place that comes to mind as still having a part of your energy and your essence

- If there are any feelings of melancholy, nostalgia, resentment, shame, or anger, allow them to be there, breathing as they flow through you

- Say to yourself, "I release this *person or place*. I reclaim what they have that is rightfully mine."

- Continue to breathe into this empowerment

PART V

Chapter 1: Back to the Basics

When most people think of mindfulness, they envision monks or yogis, sitting cross legged for hours with closed eyes and poised fingers overlooking the Himalayas. Although mindfulness is present in the lives of monks and yogis, what most people don't know is how easy it is to incorporate mindfulness into our everyday lives. As a matter of fact, a mindful state is the most natural and restful state for human beings—a state in which we were all living and moving in as children. If you think back to your childhood, you will likely remember that your concept of time and perception of reality was much different. Most children are very in touch with their emotions, letting them come and go naturally. If a child falls down in one moment and skins their knee, the child will likely begin to cry. However, if a few moments later they are being offered ice cream, their tears will dry, and they will continue on with their day. Mindfulness is the reason children are so in tune with the details of life that adults seem to miss. It is also the reason they are more likely to screech with joy, run around excitedly in enjoyable environments, wake up easily in the morning, and take the time they need to calm down from anger or sadness until the next happy moment arises. Children spend very little time thinking about things beyond the present moment. Even if they have something to look forward to, they are still likely to become invested in the moment at hand, whether that is playing, enjoying time with their parents, or eating a meal. So, what happens as people grow older that brings us away from this natural state of mindfulness?

There are a number of factors that pull people out of the present moment. From the time a child begins elementary school, they are presented with a schedule for the day, which remains relatively the same. Children are expected to remain within the structures presented to them, and the idea of forward-thinking and preparing for the next hour's activity becomes introduced. As they grow, children will likely have more expectations placed upon them, whether those expectations are academic, extracurricular, or within the home. Of course, it is necessary for children to learn how to be responsible and dedicate the time they need to the important things in life. However, as they become further exposed to the constant rush and future-oriented thinking of their parents and teachers, they come to see time as something that no longer belongs to them to fully inhabit.

Furthermore, as people approach teenage and young adulthood, they will begin to face challenges that most children are either shielded from or otherwise unaware of. People become flooded with the pressure to perform well and always be doing more today than yesterday. Although the expectations of cultures and societies vary, we can be sure that people are overwhelmed with the pressure to meet those expectations in order to be considered successful and valid. Once one bar is crossed, another one is waiting, and there is no time to slack. Additionally, the older people become, the more likely they are to be subject to long-lasting pain in their lives. This can come in the form of relationships ending, failing to accomplish something, being mistreated by other people, losing and grieving loved ones, or coming to terms with painful childhood events that did not make sense at the time. Teenagers become increasingly subject to mental health issues as they advance into adulthood, having to face all of the hard realities of the world and still come out on top. People may also be subject to trauma as a result of illness, accident, or abuse. All of these factors are enough to work against people and pull them out of the present moment, either because it is too painful to be there, or because they are simply too distracted.

Human beings experience over 60,000 thoughts per day, but the vast majority are dedicated either to planning for the future or worrying about the past. Becoming overly concerned about the future or steeping in the pains or regrets of the past can increase levels of stress in the body, which makes people more anxious and prone to physical health problems.

The mind naturally wanders, and it is impossible to keep thoughts from coming. Mindfulness is not a tool to eradicate such thoughts, as is the common misconception. Rather, it is a tool through which to acknowledge the thoughts the mind creates, bring attention to them, and allow them to move through. This ultimately brings people into what is happening here and now and gives them more control over their minds and how they orient themselves in their environments.

Because mindfulness is a skill that all human beings are equipped with at our core, it is something that can be re-learned. Just as we exercise our bodies to strengthen our muscles, so we must work to strengthen our brain through mindfulness. The way this strengthening happens is through being aware of thoughts as they arise, then breathing back into the present moment. The more practice is given to returning to the present moment, the stronger the mind will become in remaining in the present more often. Just as the body physically strengthens and becomes healthier over time with exercise, mindfulness exercises can physically change the structure of the brain to make it healthier. Mindfulness activates the positive components of the hippocampus, which is the part of the brain responsible for good things like creativity, joy, and the ability to process emotions. This, in turn, decreases stress levels, depressive tendencies, addictive behaviors, and the fight or flight instinct by shrinking the part of the brain responsible for negative things (the amygdala). Overall, increased mindfulness is the key to a longer, healthier, more creative, and more joyful life.

Chapter 2: Unlocking Your True Purpose Through Mindfulness

Re-centering Yourself

Everyone has days where everything seems to be spinning out of control, and there seems to be no way to manage the chaos. The days where you wake up late, run late to work, spill coffee on your shirt, get cut off on the road, get yelled at by your boss, spend the entire day at work in a confused frenzy, only to come home and bicker with your partner. Since the beginning of time, the human mind has been conditioned to release stress hormones and illicit the fight or flight instinct for the purpose of protection and survival. In the past, this primal instinct was very useful for escaping threats. As times have changed, the threats have become less severe, but the brain's response has remained largely the same. Now, these fight or flight reactions are likely to be triggered by everyday scenarios, such as those previously detailed. The hormone-induced responses that occur when we're stressed out are quick to send us spiraling into emotionally dramatic, and far less peaceful dimensions.

The good news is, mindfulness can be used as a tool for re-centering and gaining control over your anxiety and emotional reactions when you start to feel yourself spiral. Although there is no way to avoid stress and drama in daily life, mindfulness can serve as a shield of calm presence to protect your well-being. If you are preparing to enter a situation that you anticipate could be stressful, like a high-stakes day at work, a scary doctor's appointment, or a difficult conversation with a loved one, it can be incredibly helpful to bring yourself down to a more calm and balanced state in preparation for the stress you are about to deal with. You may find yourself with a racing heart, sweating palms, an unclear head, and the feeling of "butterflies in your stomach." Another area where it is common to feel these physical effects of anxiety is when encountering dramatic situations. Drama can arise tense moments with other people, as well as within the theoretical situations people create for themselves when worrying about what they cannot control (for example, the perception other people have of them, or events that may or may not occur in the future). Giving attention to what is happening in your mind and body and allowing yourself to breathe into the moment can be a total lifesaver in moments of drama or stress. Two to three minutes of deep breathing in your car before going to work, or taking a few deep breaths before reacting in a tense moment, can make a drastic difference in your sense of balance and your ability to deal with stress without launching into fight or flight.

Giving Your Emotions Space

The goal of mindfulness is not to eliminate emotions, but rather, to gain control over the impact they have on how we orient ourselves in the world. It is vital to honor our emotions and give them space to exist and teach us, without letting them seize control. Mindfulness is an excellent tool for giving our emotions space in this way. When an emotion arises, mindfulness gives us a chance to observe that emotion without judgment. In this calm space, we can ask our emotions, "What are you trying to teach me?" We can more clearly discern why we are experiencing a certain emotion, and become in touch with the deeper needs that may have caused that emotion to arise. Just as a child may cry when they need to be nourished our held, we may find ourselves growing angry or agitated when we need support, touch, or self-care. Similarly, we may find ourselves feeling stressed or anxious in scenarios that are subconsciously triggering moments from the past. In these cases, our stress and anxiety are begging us to become in touch with our past self, reminding ourselves that we are safe, and the traumatic moments from the past are over. Once our emotions have been given a non-judgmental space to exist, they can smoothly and peacefully move through the body and be released. This frees us to move from moment to moment like children do, without being constrained by unresolved emotions. Additionally, giving this space to our emotions in mindfulness helps to temper our reactions, which can prevent us from acting out in extreme ways and potentially doing or saying something we regret.

Making Clear Decisions

With the human mind constantly being muddled with thoughts, it can be hard to see things clearly. Sometimes our minds are cluttered by the expectations flying at us from every different direction, or perhaps by our fears of what will happen if things don't go to plan. When it comes to making decisions, we are often faced with numerous options, and it can be difficult to navigate through the chaos in our minds to come to a well thought out resolution. In a distracted, anxious, or removed state, our minds are like a pond on a rainy day—rippling to a point where there is no more clarity. Mindfulness is the calming of the waters, which brings us to a place where we can more clearly think of all possible outcomes of a decision and check in with what we truly need before moving into the next moment.

Keeping Yourself Safe

Although fight or flight instincts originally developed as a way to keep humans safe, in many modern-day scenarios, they do quite the opposite. Let's go back to the example from the beginning of the chapter about the chain of events in a typical chaotic day. If you wake up late in the morning and rush to make your coffee, not paying attention to what you are doing, you run the risk of haphazardly screwing the lid on your to-go cup, then sloshing boiling hot coffee over the edge of the cup and onto yourself as you bolt out the door. Although such a scenario could simply result in a stained shirt, the inattentiveness could have a more drastic effect, such as burning yourself or someone else. Driving to work in a state of panic over running late causes you to be more likely to break the rules of the road— driving too fast, making dangerous decisions when changing lanes, taking turns too fast, running yellow lights just before they turn red, etc. Additionally, the panicked state can lead to anger with yourself or others on the road, which can further impair judgment and put you at greater risk of an accident. Attempting to have a conversation with your boss if you are in fight or flight mode could result in being overly emotional and saying or doing something extreme which could place you at odds within your workplace, potentially even costing your position. Going throughout your day in a frenzy causes you to be less aware of what is going on around you, which can lead to further threats to safety like leaving a burner on, forgetting to eat or drink enough water, or neglecting those in your care (such as pets or children) as a result of your own inner distractions. Finally, as stress from the day carries into the home at the end of the day, it can pose a major threat to relationships. The more stressed out and less clear thinking you are, the more likely you are to say or do something threatening to your partner, to put yourself in an aggressive and volatile situation, and to make brash decisions that have the potential to haunt your future.

Improving Relationships

Just as we must give ourselves space to learn, grow, and process our experiences, we must give that space to those around us as well. When a partner or friend is acting in a way we don't enjoy, mindfulness can allow us to take a step back and look at the situation from a position of empathy. We can allow ourselves to hold space for whatever that person may be going through individually and express our support while also maintaining boundaries and staying in control of what we can. Everyone is deserving of space to be listened to, understood, and supported for who they are. However, it is incredibly difficult to give that space to anyone if it has not been cleared within oneself.

When we operate out of a mindless state, there is hardly any space to meet our own needs and process our own experience, much less to provide that to other people. This can lead us to be closed off to the ones we love, push them away, or act out in anger, selfishness, or aggression. If we have not given space to what is going on within us, we cannot offer full empathy to others. Only 20% of the population is recorded to practice true empathy, which can be linked to the rarity of true mindfulness among adults. Mindfulness allows us to be more present to our own needs in order to hold adequate space for the needs of others as well.

Attention and mutual respect are core elements of every functional relationship. Practicing mindfulness can improve relationships with all the people in our lives by preparing us for every engagement and calming our minds enough to be fully present in the moments we share with others. Mindfulness clears the space for us to listen intentionally to other people and pay more attention to what kind of people they are and what kind of support they need. It allows us to love other people better by increasing our awareness of how they feel most loved. By being present in the moment at hand, as opposed to trapped in the past or future, you are more likely to remember to pick up the phone and give your grandmother a call, to be fully engaged when interacting with your child, or to remember the kind of kombucha your significant other likes best from the store. Not only does mindfulness allow for more meaningful conversations and joyful memories, but it also increases the functionality of our relationships overall so that both ourselves and those we love are feeling fully respected, listened to, and encouraged.

Fostering True Joy

We often hear the term "childlike joy" to describe moments of pure bliss, enthusiasm, and full satisfaction. As people grow into adults, such moments tend to be few and far between, with many remembering the most joyful moments to have been those that occurred in childhood. The expectations of daily life become too much, and most people find themselves trapped in a cycle of constant anticipation. People spend so much time thinking about where they would rather be (on vacation, in bed, enjoying the weekend) that the days melt into each other without us realizing all the moments of our lives we are missing. The biggest societal misconception is that true happiness lies in what we do not yet have. We are flooded with lies such as "Once I can buy this new TV, then I'll be happy," or, "Once I have a partner, then I'll be happy," or, "I'll be happy once I can say I've been to five different countries." Mindfulness abolishes these lies by proving to us that the capacity for true joy lies not in the future but in the here and now. Wherever you are right now, whatever you have, and whichever stage of life you're in, mindfulness reminds you that *this* is your chance to experience beauty and satisfaction like never before. Take time to look at the flowers you did not notice growing in front of your neighbor's house, the complexity of coffee's flavor as it slides down your throat, the way your loved one's eyes crinkle when they smile, the laughter of a child, every intricate flavor of dinner, or the unique people wandering up and down the streets you drive every day to work. It is here that joy resides; all you have to do is be present enough to recognize it.

Chapter 3: Moving Mindfully in Daily Life

Coming to the Present Moment: Daily Guided Mindfulness Meditation With Journaling (Week 1)

Cultivating Mindfulness

This meditation should be done in a space where you feel fully comfortable, safe, and relaxed. Perhaps it is in a corner of your bedroom, in a garden, by your favorite lake, or even in your car. Make sure you can fully relax and avoid distractions. Some people meditate best with instrumental music or nature sounds in the background, while others prefer silence. Feel free to try multiple methods and see which is most soothing to you (this can vary depending on the day). You may do this meditation sitting in a chair, on a mat, or lying flat on your back with your palms up to the sky. You will need to give yourself 5-20 minutes of time to practice, depending on your skill level and current state. If you like, you can set a timer.

Start by coming into the moment with a few deep breaths. Settle into your body and take note of any sensations you feel. If you feel pain, tingling, warmth, or tightness in any part of your body, focus your breath into that space. Imagine any tension unfurling into openness. Notice as your thoughts arise. Take notice of them, then allow them to pass as you come back to the breath. If it is helpful, you can try a breathing pattern in order to culminate focus. To do the 4-4-4 breathing pattern, breathe in for 4 counts, hold for 4 counts, and breathe out for 4 counts. To do the 5-5-7 breathing pattern, breath in for 5 counts, hold for 5 counts, release for 7 counts. Sometimes it helps to imagine breathing in the things you wish to see more of in your daily life (creativity, love, patience, openness) and exhale the negative things (fear, negativity, sadness, stress). Allow yourself to spend a few moments in a more active state of breathing in, releasing, and paying attention to your body.

With practice, you may enter a state where your thoughts slow and you become fully grounded in the present moment. In this state, you are no longer bombarded with thoughts, nor distracted by elements of your environment. It becomes easier to return to the breath. All restlessness and tension in the body seem to melt away, and the mind reaches a flowing, liquified state. There may be days when you cannot enter into this state, and you remain restless throughout the course of the meditation. If this happens, allow it to be that way, observing every thought that arises, then letting it go.

After the time is up, begin to arrive in the moment by moving your body slightly—wiggling your fingers and toes, tensing and releasing your muscles, etc. Next, you're your eyes. Notice how bright and clear the world looks to mindful eyes. Notice the calm, transcendent feeling in your body, and continue to move with it as you go about your day.

Mindfulness Meditation Journal Prompt (Week 1):

What did you feel in your body before beginning? What do you feel now?

Which thoughts continued to arise in your consciousness? Could these thoughts have been trying to teach you something or speak to a deeper need you may have?

How does the world look after opening your eyes? What do you notice?

Come back after going about your day for several hours. Did you bring mindfulness with you into the world? If so, how?

Coming to the Present Moment: Daily Guided Mindfulness Meditation With Journaling (Week 2)

Taking Mindfulness Into the World

This meditation will be done with your eyes open in moments if your daily life. This is not a specific meditation you have to set aside time for, but rather a state you come into. Notice where your attention goes in a given moment. If your attention is drawn to a particular sight, like the nearest tree or a view from the top of a mountain, allow yourself to see it fully. Repeatedly tell yourself, "see, see, see." Breathe as you allow your eyes to truly become totally focused and take in the image fully, allowing it to become a part of your awareness.

If your attention is drawn to an auditory experience, such as the sound of cars on a city street, a rushing body of water, or an internal monologue, give full attention to that thing. Soak in that auditory experience, breathing slowly and telling yourself, "hear, hear, hear."

You may also be drawn to a particular physical or emotional experience within the body. This experience may be positive, like a pleasant bodily sensation or a feeling of joy. It may also be negative, like physical pain, or feelings of anger or feel. Either way, allow yourself to become fully present with what is there, breathing into the experience and seeing what it has to teach you. Breathe into that bodily experience, telling yourself, "feel, feel, feel."

Throughout the day, you'll find that your attention is pulled in various directions. Mindfulness is the choice to tune in to whichever place you're going in a given moment and give full attention to that experience for whatever it is.

Mindfulness Meditation Journal Prompt (Week 2):

How difficult was it to bring mindfulness into your daily life in this way? Where did you face the most challenges?

Did your attention tend towards certain experiences (visual, auditory, bodily) more than others?

Describe a specific moment where you brought mindfulness to your experience and felt truly present. What did you observe?

Coming to the Present Moment: Daily Guided Mindfulness Meditation With Journaling (Week 3)

Mindfulness at Work (or School)

The first part of this meditation should happen in a place outside of work, where you feel safe, calm, and separated from the issues you may face in the workplace. Start by identifying your biggest struggles at work. The journal portion will give you a space to write them down. Do you struggle with productivity? Boredom? Stress? Conflict resolution? Work relationships? Once you have identified your most significant area(s) of struggle, close your eyes and visualize what that unpleasant experience looks like. Perhaps it looks like you, rushing around mindlessly like a bee in a hive, stressed out and too overbooked to step away and breathe because there are more calls to make, more e-mails to send, more things to do. Or, perhaps it is the co-worker, professor, or boss that makes your stomach drop whenever you think about having to interact with them. Perhaps you feel unfulfilled at work and find yourself constantly checking the clock, thinking about the moment you get to leave. Maybe you have so many things to do and no idea where to start, so you waste a lot of time on mindless tasks. Whatever your struggles at work are, use your time and space away from work to safely visualize the situation. Breathe into the mental circumstance.

As you breathe, begin to envision what this experience would look like if it went the way you want it to. Perhaps it looks like the mental clarity that allows you to know exactly what needs to get done and how to make the best possible use of your time. It could be a greater sense of calm and courage when talking with your difficult boss or co-worker and having your message be well-received on their end. It may also be a deeper sense of satisfaction and enjoyment in the work you're doing, providing you the ability to step back and feel a sense of joy with where you're at, without constantly thinking about the next thing. Reframe the moment in your mind until you've created a mental space that feels good. Let yourself sit there, breathing, soaking it in for several minutes.

Once you go into the workplace (or school), you can bring this meditation into your life by going back to the peaceful mental image you've created over and over again. When you begin to feel stressed, bored, anxious, or unproductive, return to the space where you do not feel those things. Bring that energy into your daily work life, and watch how it revolutionizes your experience.

Mindfulness Meditation Journal Prompt (Week 3):

What do you identify as your biggest challenge(s) at work or school?

How does it look when you reframe your struggles to create a positive mental image?

What do you observe about bringing this positive mental image into difficult situations in the workplace or at school?

Mini Meditation Toolbox: 15 Quick and Easy Meditations to Integrate Mindfulness Into Your Daily Life

One-Minute Mindfulness

- Find a space where you can be alone, like on your bathroom break or in your car right before going into work, school, or home at the end of the day.

- Set a timer for one minute

- Close your eyes and focus exclusively on your breathing

- Take notice of the stresses, thoughts, and anxieties that arise, then let them go

- When you open your eyes, notice how you feel de-stressed, clear-minded, and prepared to go about your upcoming tasks and interactions with others

5-Minute Body Scan

- Set a timer for 5 minutes (if needed)

- Close your eyes and take several deep, cleansing breaths. You may use the 4-4-4 or 5-5-7 breathing patterns to deepen the breath

- Begin to bring attention to your body

- Take notice of any sensations that arise-- warmth, tingling, tension, etc.

- Bring your attention to the soles of the feet. Tighten your muscles by curling your toes, then release. What sensations do you feel?

- Continue moving up the body to your calves, hips, abdomen, chest, hands, arms, face, and neck. Observe any sensations that arise, and breathe into those sensations.
- Tighten and release the muscles in each of these areas, allowing any pent-up energy or resistance to be released
- Feel your body become grounded, relaxing completely into the floor, bed, or chair as you come into the present moment in your body and all tension melts away

Mindful Bath/Shower (10-minute meditation)

- As you begin your bath or shower, take a moment to breathe. Remove yourself from the stresses of the day and allow yourself to re-center
- Bring attention to each part of your body as you wash it
- Take notice of any sensations you feel as you move from the soles of your feet to the ends of your hair
- Breathe in the pleasant scent of the soaps and the warmth of the water. Allow yourself to feel clean, warm, and safe.
- As you wash each part of your body, thank it for what it does for you. Then, thank yourself for taking care of your body.

Mindful Morning Routine (15-30 minutes)

- Before getting out of bed, begin to stretch gently, letting thoughts come and go as your mind and body wake up. Do not rush yourself.

- Once you are ready to get out of bed, bring your attention to the space around you and the day ahead. Feel yourself become fully present in that space and prepared to move mindfully through your day

- Pay attention to every move you make, from putting on clothes, to washing your face, to setting the water on the stove to boil.

- Cultivate your awareness for the day ahead by moving slowly and calmly, one task at a time, becoming fully awake to the world

Mindful Housekeeping

- Allow yourself to become focused on the task at hand and only that task. Let every other thing you have to do or think about fade into the background.

- Bring your attention to the breath and the specific way your body moves as you complete a particular task or chore

- Give space to any thoughts or emotions that arise in your consciousness, allowing yourself to process them in a mindful state

Mindful Sit-and-Drink (10-minute meditation)

- Find a calm, quiet space where you can sit and observe the world around you (preferably outside or near a window looking outside)
- Pour a glass of your favorite tea, coffee, or cocktail to enjoy
- Eliminate all distractions. Draw your attention to the intricate flavors of the drink, and the pleasure of pulling something you enjoy into your body
- Take notice of the things happening around you. Find the things in the environment that bring you the most peace, and allow their presence with you to help you calm your mind. Become completely indulged in the moment.

Mindful Scheduling (10-minute meditation)

- Sit down with a pen and paper and center yourself with five deep breaths.
- Think about the days to come. Consider your priorities, remembering that every task is significant and an opportunity for increased mindfulness
- Ask yourself, "Am I giving myself adequate time to bring mindfulness and intentionality into each of these activities?"
- Take notice of any activities you feel you won't be able to be fully present for. Consider taking a thing or two off the list and saving them for a better time.
- Take notice of any feelings of stress, nervousness, or rush you feel in regards to your schedule. Breathe into those feelings.

- As you continue to write your schedule, allow yourself to feel empowered, in control, and prepared to be mindful of everything you are about to do

Mindful Driving

- Leave the house with plenty of time to be relaxed and focused. After entering the car, take a few moments to breathe and center yourself
- Once you start to drive, begin to take note of the things passing by. What do you see today that you did not see yesterday?
- Breathe in your visual surroundings, using them to center and remind yourself: "I am here. I am in this community. This is my life, and I am awake to it."

Mindful Walking (10-20-minute meditation)

- Choose an area where you can relax and bring attention to your surroundings. This can be in a park, in the city, on the beach, in your neighborhood, etc.
- Set out on your walk with no distractions
- Take notice of the things your eyes fall upon. If something specific catches your attention, allow yourself to pause and breathe it in.
- Pay attention to the sounds that surround you, giving yourself space to truly hear them

- Pay attention to the feeling of your feet on the pavement, the swing of your arms at your sides, and the rhythm of your breath
- Let your heart expand in curiosity and openness to whatever is ready to meet you in this space
- Allow yourself to become totally saturated with your surroundings, remembering that everything you see, hear, and feel is a part of you

Mindful Cooking and Eating

- As you enter the kitchen to prepare food, take a moment to center yourself in the moment with a few deep breaths
- Give every moment of the cooking process your full attention, from washing, to cutting, to cooking. Become fully immersed in the process (you can do this even with simple meals, like mindfully spreading peanut butter on bread)
- Breathe loving-kindness into the cooking process, remembering that the food you make will provide nourishment to yourself and others
- Once the food is ready, clear the eating space of distractions. Avoid multi-tasking
- Chew every bite of food 20-30 times, letting yourself be engulfed in the flavor and practicing gratitude for the nourishment
- Walk away from your meal feeling truly nourished and renewed

Mindful Waiting

- The next time you're trying to distract yourself at the doctor's office, the mechanic, or waiting for a friend or colleague to arrive, remind yourself that waiting is one of the most sacred times to engage in mindfulness

- Breathe into the moment, becoming aware of what surrounds you

- Bring awareness to your body. How are you feeling? Take note of any sensations

- Become aware of the thoughts that come once you stop numbing yourself with distractions. What things are running through your mind?

- Pay attention to the deeper thoughts you may have previously been ignoring. Ask yourself what you can learn about yourself and your life, or if there are any actions you need to take.

Mindful Creativity (at least 5 minutes)

- Set aside anywhere from five minutes to several hours of undivided time

- Engage in a creative project like art, writing, dancing, etc.

- Bring full presence to the creative project and try to eliminate all expectations. Allow the moment to carry you.

- Pay attention to how your mind and body react as the moment carries you. How do you feel?

- Examine what you create as a result of this free-flowing creativity

Mindful Play

- Dedicate time each week to doing something truly fun—something that makes you feel like a kid again (climbing a tree, swimming in the lake, drawing with chalk, baking cookies, having a game night, etc.)

- Eliminate all distractions and allow this to be a moment to step away from your everyday life and responsibilities

- Allow yourself to become lost in the childlike joy of play. Laugh loudly, let your body dance, be curious.

- Let the feeling of childlike joy saturate your body and carry this joy with you as you move back into your daily life.

Mindful Movement (10-30 minutes)

- Choose one of your favorite forms of movement (swimming, walking, dancing, going to the gym, etc.) and dedicate at least ten minutes to it

- As you begin to move, establish a deeper sense of body awareness. Pay attention to the feelings in your body as you begin to warm up and exercise

- Pay attention to the way your heart beats, your lungs heave, your face begins to sweat, and your body tingles with the sense of being alive

- Thank your body for all it does for you.

Mindful Listening/Quality Time

- Apply this meditation to any quality time you spend with another person, whether that is grabbing coffee or going for a walk with a loved one, interacting with co-workers, are conversing with the grocery store cashier

- Before interacting with others, bring attention to your levels of empathy. Set the intention to hold space for other people and the moments you share with them

- Eliminate distractions (like technology) and allow yourself to put everything else going on in your life on pause in order to be fully present

- One of the best ways to show love for people and to cultivate personal mindfulness is through mindful listening. Focus all of your attention on the other person and what they are saying. When you ask how their day is going, be present to hear the answer.

- Do not think of what your next move will be, what you will say, or where you will go. Simply be there, showing loving-kindness, holding space, and taking it all in.

Mini Meditation Toolbox: 10 Quick and Easy Meditations to Ease Stress, Depression, Addiction, Anxiety, Pain, Distraction, and Loss Using Mindfulness

Journaling the Consciousness (10-minute meditation)

- Sit down with a journal and a pen and set your timer for 10 minutes
- As thoughts, worries, or emotions arise, immediately write them down. Do not worry about structure, grammar, or content, just write.
- When the time is up, look over what you wrote
- Ask yourself which themes seem to reoccur. Where are you feeling stress in your life? What is occupying most of your mental space?
- Close your eyes and take a few moments to breathe and meditate on the thing(s) that need your attention the most
- Open your eyes. Notice how you feel lighter and in touch with your experience

Distraction Cleanse: Clearing the Space in your Mind

- *Find a quiet place and begin to breathe*
- Ask yourself: "What is distracting me from being present right now?"
- Give space to that distraction, whether it is an invasive thought, personal emotion, or someone else's emotion

- Say to yourself: "I am letting my distractions move through me as I ground myself in the present moment. Nothing is more important than right now."

- Breathe until you feel the distraction melt away into presence and mental clarity.

Re-Writing the Moment: A Short Meditation to Ease Emotional Pain of the Past

- Sit down with a journal and a pen and set your timer for 1 minute

- Take this 1 minute to write down any moment(s) of the past which have caused you a lot of pain

- After the minute is up, choose one of the painful moments, close your eyes, and begin to imagine the moment in a safe way. Be sure to keep breathing.

- When you open your eyes, take your pen and paper and re-imagine the painful moment. What do you wish had happened? How do you wish you could think about the moment now?

- After re-imagining the painful moment, remind yourself that this is a new moment. Everyone has painful memories, but you do not have to stay in spaces of the past, which are painful for you.

- Close your eyes, take a few more breaths, and say to yourself, "I release the pain of that moment of the past. This is a new moment, and I will move with it."

Re-claiming your Inner Power: A Short Meditation to Face Addiction

- Breathe into the moment, allowing yourself to think about the implications your addiction has on your life

- Without judgment, question your addiction. Ask yourself, "What has been left empty in me that I am trying to fill with this?" Listen for any emotions or past experiences of trauma, grief, or abandonment that arise. Allow them to be there.

- Say to yourself, "Now that I understand the root of my addiction, I can begin to be set free."

- With closed eyes, begin to breathe. With each breath, imagine your addiction's hold on you weakening and weakening until eventually, you have been released.

- Move forward into your life with the idea that your addiction's hold on you is loosening, day by day.

Letter to the Lost: A Short Meditation to Address Grief and Loss

- Sit down with a journal and a pen and take five deep breaths to bring you into the moment

- Allow someone you have lost to come to mind. This can be a relationship that has ended, someone who has died, etc.

- Close your eyes and breathe into the space this person has left empty within you. Allow yourself to experience any emotions that arise.

- When you open your eyes, take a few minutes to write what you wish you could have said to that person

- After you have finished your letter, close your eyes again. Tell your grief that it is okay for it to be there. With every breath, imagine yourself moving forward in your life, released from every regret you may have with someone you've lost

In with The Positive, Out with the Negative: A Short Breathing Technique

- Find a comfortable space and prepare to use the 5-5-7 breathing technique
- Breathe in for five counts and think of something positive you want to bring into this moment (kindness, peace, wisdom, etc.)
- Hold for five counts, allowing this positive thing to fill your body
- Exhale for seven counts, thinking of something negative you want to release from your body in this moment (stress, tension, selfishness, etc.)
- Begin again with a second emotion. Do this as many times as you like until you feel well-equipped with positive emotions and have released all negative ones

Space to Breathe: A Short Meditation to Gain Control over your Anxiety

- When you begin to feel anxious, step away, take a breath, and ground yourself in the moment by finding one thing you can see, one thing you can hear, and one thing you can feel. Focus deeply on each thing.

- Allow your anxiety space to exist. Remember, anxiety is the reaction your emotional brain has when it senses a threat. You can bring yourself back from catastrophe mode by using the rational brain to repeatedly remind yourself: "I am safe. I am in control. I am capable of being calm."

- Keep breathing and saying these rational-brained affirmations until you begin to feel your anxiety melt away

- Move into the next moment feeling calm, anxiety-free, and empowered

Emotion Coding: A Short Meditation to Bring you in Touch with your Emotions

- Find a quiet, comfortable place where you can easily connect with yourself

- Close your eyes and breathe deeply (you may use a breathing pattern if desired)

- Begin to travel inwards. Say to yourself, "I am ready to accept the emotions that are here."

- Wait patiently, focusing on the breath, and observing every emotion that rises to the surface.

- When an emotion arises, ask yourself a series of questions:

  1. "Is this emotion mine or someone else's?"
  2. "Does this emotion serve me or hold me back?"
  3. "What is this emotion trying to teach me?"
  4. "Should I release this emotion or put it into action?"

- When it comes to answering each question, listen to your intuition. The answers to each question are already within you. Do not question your natural answers.

- If you are being told to release an old or negative emotion, or an emotion that belongs to someone else, breathe and imagine it melting away with every exhale

- If you are being told to foster a positive emotion or a strong emotion that can create positive change in the world, sit with that, breathing, and being open to how that emotion can be useful.

The "I Love..." Gratitude Meditation (2-minute meditation)

- Find a private space, preferably one in front of a mirror
- Start a timer for 2 minutes
- For two minutes, speak out loud sentences of gratitude beginning with the words "I love..." ("I love my partner," "I love coffee," "I love my cat," "I love sunflowers," I love my mom," "I love to dance," "I love that I am healthy,").
- Say as many things as you can, one after the other. Do not think too much, simply let the things you love flow from your lips
- When the timer goes off, look in the mirror and say "And I love you," to yourself
- Feel the magic of gratitude transforming your life, your self-confidence, and your ability to be mindful

The Mindful Manifestation: A Short Meditation to Manifest what you Want in Life

- Sit down with a journal and pen

- Begin to cultivate mindfulness by bringing attention to your breath and any sensations in your body

- Ask yourself the question: "What do I want most in life?"

- As the answers start to come, open your eyes and begin to write your desires with the words "I manifest…" in front of them ("I manifest empathy." "I manifest peace of mind." "I manifest protection." "I manifest safety." "I manifest love." "I manifest awareness." "I manifest wisdom." "I manifest pure joy.")

- With each manifestation, close your eyes, and say it to yourself at least three times. Feel this manifestation become a part of your reality.